Ńchéfù Road

Poems by Uche Ogbuji

ŃCHÉFÙ ROAD

POEMS BY

UCHE OGBUJI

First published in 2022
An Eyewear Publishing book, The Black Spring Press Group
Grantully Road, Maida Vale, London w9
United Kingdom

Typesetting User Design, Illustration and Typesetting, UK
Cover art Obinna "Igbobinna NSB" Eze
Author photo Melissa Rich Design, Boulder, Colorado

The author has requested the publisher use American spelling
and grammar wherever possible in this edition

ISBN-13 978-1-913606-93-0

By Mel Pryor

Ńchéfù Road caught my attention on first reading and didn't disappoint on further readings. "Run your languages this way; I want all your words/And their secrets, pick locks to your treasure chest;" sings the poem "Run it!" and this desire for "words" and "their secrets" brings to mind Pablo Neruda: You can say anything you want, alright, but it's the words that sing, they soar and descend…I bow to them…I cling to them, I run them down…I love words so much…The unexpected ones…The ones I wait for greedily or stalk until, suddenly, they drop…Vowels I love…They glitter like coloured stones, they leap like silver fish… Everything exists in the word.

Ńchéfù Road delights in words and in language. "Ńchéfù" is the Igbo word for "amnesia, forgetfulness," and the collection is both a remembrance of the narrator's past, as far as memory allows it, and a coming to terms with a heritage marked by violence and displacement. Igbo allusions and folklore and words (the Igbo word "ényí" for "elephant," we learn, is a visual but not an aural rhyme of the Igbo word "ényì" for "friend") sit comfortably among resonances of canonical English poetry. Derek Walcott says he never separated the writing of poetry from prayer, and this collection opens with a poem/prayer like an incantation.

Any moralizing feels more playfully affectionate and benevolent than didactic, and the unexpected juxtapositions, unobtrusive humour, seductive sounds, musicality and line energy suggest the multiplicity of perception at work in this wonderful, exuberant collection.

Dedicated to my father, Dr. Linus Thomas-Ogbuji and mother, Mrs. Margaret Ogbuji, R.N., both of whom fought for the nation of Biafra, and after losing that fight went abroad without a farthing in their pockets to establish our family.

Further dedicated to

Dr. Nnamdi Azikiwe, Zik of Africa, founding father of Nigeria and of the University of Nigeria, Nsukka (Great Lions and Lionesses, *kwenu!*)

Col. Odumegwu Ojukwu, Ikemba of Nnewi, leader of the proud but short-lived nation of Biafra (*Ényímbà Ényí, Ñzọ̀gbú-Ñzọ̀gbú!*).

Christopher Okigbo, icon of African poetry, brave soldier for Biafra's cause ("This day belongs to a miracle of thunder").

In special recognition of

Wọlé Ṣóyíinká, who risked his own neck with both sides of the Biafra war, in the name of friendship, and in the desperate hope for peace.

May my words brush the merest hem of your legacy, elders. Guide my steps backward and forward along Ńchéfù road.

    —Uche Ogbuji

CONTENTS

Orison   13

1 Azikiwe   17

A Sixteen for Dr. Nnamdi Azikiwe   19
Canal   20
Ọpụ̀tá na Ọ̀mụ̀gwọ́   24
Mango Flesh   28
Colossus   29
Ụ́mụ̀ Dí Ụ́zụ́ (Smith's Posterity)   30
Electron Microscopy   34
     I   34
     II   35
     III   36
     IV   37
Why should I Murmur?   38
At the University of Port Harcourt Teaching Hospital   41
Ogbúnàbàlị̀ and Hypnos, 1949   43
Mysteries of Harvest: Home   46
Two Kitchens   47
Run it!   48

2 Ojukwu   53

A Sixteen for Col. Ojukwu   55
Ǹzọ̀gbú-Ǹzọ̀gbú   56
Ravenant   62
Mysteries of Harvest II   65
Ikot Abasi Mbong   66
Fish Eyed Jonahs   68
Elephant Head [Ísí Ényí]   72

Okobi and the Crying... 74

    I 74

    II 74

Rheotype 76

Who, Lumumba? 78

3 Okigbo 81

A Sixteen for Christopher Okigbo 83

Éké 84

Faceful of Rain 86

Jungle Buffalo 90

Le Freak Musique Afrique 92

Two-Voiced Flute 96

Mystic Drummalogue 98

Fortune of Chí 101

Road to Onitsha, 1989 102

Road from Calabar to Abuja 106

Rainbow City Presage of Storm 108

Ìgbò Directions in Amsterdam 111

Dear Bonny, Dear Biafara, 113

Prayer Before Writing 114

A Sixteen for the Diaspora 115

4 Ńchéfù Road 117

Ńchéfù Road 119

    I 119

    II 120

    III 123

    IV 125

    V 127

    VI 129

    VII 131

    VIII 132

    IX 134

    X 136

Notes

Notes   **139**

    I Azikiwe   139

    II Ojukwu   140

    III Okigbo   141

    IV Ńchéfù Road   143

Acknowledgments   145

ORISON

She pressed the message against the flattened sole of my right foot
Àlà
She may have loosed her clutch control of Ụmụ̀ézèàlàíhú
Àlà
But she has gained dominion worldwide with her seed on trade wind
Àlà
She warned me never to skulk the bush paths at night alone
Ọ̀kpàngú
I heard her and paced my turf by train, plane and motorcar
Àlà
She warned me never to neglect my barns in laziness
Ọ̀kpàngú
I heard her and mastered the earthless crop of abstract symbols
Àlà
She warned: never leave your children near fire or deep water
Ọ̀kpàngú
I heard her and nurtured them in purple mountaineering
Àlà
"I think, my son, you have quite confused my meanings", she says
Àlà

Goddess, you know that I shall return, my children with me
Ìséé
A new worldly wife as well for Ụmụ̀ézèàlàíhú
Ìséé
Pursue from my heading the demon madman chimpanzee
Ọ̀kpàngú
If he comes wrestling lend me grim force of young heart
    failure
Ọ̀kpàngú

Send me triple masquerade of my space age ancestors
Azikiwe
Send me insistence kilned into my muscle and bone
Ojukwu
Send me miracle of thunder with all thrills it echoes
Okigbo
Those things I've forgotten be my sacrifice to you
Àlà
They'll do for blessings those few things left in my memory.
Ìséé!

1/ AZIKIWE

A SIXTEEN FOR DR. NNAMDI AZIKIWE

To the tune of Souls of Mischief — '93 til Infinity
[A-Plus, with love to Billy Cobham]

The great Zik of Africa, pan-African legend and 1st president of Nigeria.
From 1960 'til the Biafran dream, in reality until an infinity where
nationalism finally dies an overdue death

Who had the passion to take action, work out the factions
Get us traction for the black man's satisfaction
The goons split us out from the room, Benin and Cameroon
Colonial ghouls with their pantaloons and barracoons.
So green/white/green's what Zik of Africa fought for
Pen of independence, he was editor and author
Medals as a swimmer, a runner and a boxer
Three-continent athlete plus an academic doctor.
Man of the people spoke Hausa, Yoruba, Igbo
Different cultures; it's the same red we bleed, though
You talk I listen; you listen, I talk
40 degrees in the kitchen, friction keeping us hot
But we've got to find a way to build in this adversity
So Lions and Lionesses have their university
The first on the scene, person whose dream keeps nursing me
Creed of the Zik is key to what my verses mean.

CANAL

First river from which all other rivers.
First road from which all other roads.
2:45am, Nov 2, 1970

The beat swept left as walls whaled away at him,
Squeezing him head forward of feet, the beat
That used to keep two stroke boom bap on the reg
Now rolled in with spasm polyrhythmic.
No Jonah, that one, nor any like him,
He was to be anointed by his host
Not by some god who spoke old okey-doke
To red-capped elders of his host's dumbness.
One he knew only from the inside blessed him;
She his universe made his laws of physics,
Firstly made his means to break them, graded him
Silver surfer towards the wormhole cervix.

A new universe swam in as hosannahs
Swung from voices barely bold enough to brush
Syllables with two shushing lips of les bises,
Voices in muted but indubitably
Slick cypher spit of beatbox wow and warble.
Having lost the deep red leavings of sun
From the skinflint window of his grotto,
From the cave where he played veiled-in Proteus,
From basecamp for his days of shapeshifting,
Having descended in stark innocence,
Tumbling into dun before the dawning,
He tried on the new things he was hearing,
Patched his fears into the nightmare palaver.

How did he know that as soon as he choked
The one track amniotic clear of his throat,
He would freak the fit out, shrieking in tongues?
He somehow sensed how many languages
The coming world would hurl his boomerang way.
He didn't even really know what light was
Yet he would come out loud to those who listened
Like: "Yes Goethe, I am your apothanatic!
I say Mehr Licht! Mehr Licht! and let there be!"

Ticking down to big bang of the starfire sense
His eyes tingled in their million receptors,
Their rod upon nerve upon nerve upon cone.
Stoked with the blinded human body's hunger
Craving his promised soup of personal morning.
Out of mother's rich tidepool of life water,
Approaching the surface, a cloud of vision
Awaited early refraction to ignite it.

This was foretaste of sight marbled in sound,
This garrulous ward of what he would learn
Was an Ikot Ene hospital, St. Joseph's,
Woofing tweets of voice he'd learn were inflected
With collegial regard for his gifted
Midwife Sister Superior of a mother.

They welled whoopsa boy-o-boy! as the breach
Oozed him from the narrow within time's arrow—
The cosmic opposite event horizon.
His one degree of freedom, scratch that, half that,
Opened into frightful three space where other
And other and other crammed in on him,
Lit up his senses with blistering hazards.
He could blink but he couldn't cup his ears.

The funk of post-war highlife soaked him through,
His eyes dancing up strobe and disco ball.

He had rappelled to ground, away from cliff face
Of netherlife and now that he could behold
What prusik he used, it turned out to be
Our sun star at tropical full tilt and all
The noise said sun inspires, irruptive
Babel just after dawn in the marketplace,
Wetin dey before haba! and wahala.
Letting go the tether meant letting in
The rest: the sniffed taste and the throb-along touch.

Turned out his chí was that very rope-knot,
The anchor high in the depths between worlds
Signaling diminuendo down the wire
Of umbilical antenna. Chí said:

This is where we must part ways in order to be joined for life.
Mother will one day want you cottoning to pentecost,
You're about to properly meet her—will she persuade you?
Father will beg you bid the holy spirit: you there! Get lost!
He'll wire you for science to chant down supernova fire
On basilica walls left by colonial kill-and-go.
Feeling opposed, they won't have expected their split sacrifice
To serve the alchemy that makes for crown thorn oil of di egwu.
You will live with your head in flames, yet sight lines at freezing.
Cool it to tune hold in each moment, the easier for seizing.

With that last flash-bang of mystery he woke
To sense of hands kneading him for commerce,
To cough up that foretold down payment,
Spent wet medium of his lungs in exchange
For fresh purchase of breath to take within.

This was proof they needed that he could deal,
Proof enough for them to knock off the slapping,
Needle drop to the scratch, fingertips down
On vinyl black to two-tone his move on groove,
To set him back upon that old school beat
So long in the rocking, set him on her chest,
That cello chamber of her voice tempo down
His stress. Forty-five all nerve and jump-jive
Now spinning sweet breeze thirty-three and a third
Under novel influence of her arm hold,
Eye to eye, first thickly-milk to thirsty mouth.

Narrow enough in the choking was the road
That opened to all new things, but just so,
Too broad with excess until he once again
Found the muted magic in every moment.

Here's his first story. He forgets, yet he is well,
First comfort always with him, albeit missing—
Never missing. Sweet mother. Always with him.
This first comfort shall be the ultimate.
He forgets. All is forgotten. All is well.

ỌPÙTÁ NA ỌMÙGWỌ́

I no go forget you / for de suffer wey you suffer for me—eh!

—Prince Nico Mbarga, "Sweet Mother"

Reader, I was born to defy you,
If you are a certain sort of god.
I move that I surrender shape
What can you seize of a pseudopod?

I was newborn in the compounds
That drew my mother's people south,
A modest foothold in Calabar
At Cross River's worldly mouth.

Father had just left for Cairo,
Shrugging off old echoes, horns of war;
He'd learned word of the new patriarchs:
Would he wager on earthier lore?

Umune, goddess of the womb,
Who stands for human origin,
Is in extremis refuge
From mortal tragedy, ruin or sin.

Mother's birthing vantage point
Was ancestral Ikot Ana;
Swollen, she made her way south from
Her workplace of Abagana.

A crossroads is a fluid moment,
Stirring one world into another—
The soldier cools, two years at peace;
Midwife adept becomes a mother.

Ikot Ana looks west across
Her river to Ohafia
And Arochukwu, ghost warpaths
Through red earth, rains and raffia.

Mum isn't Ìgbò but she knows
The forested passage to the sea
That brought Dad's kin then swept them off:
Adventure, trade and slavery.

Ụ̀mụ̀ ńné are my mother's blood
(Umon gives them a different name):
Their hand versus Dad's act hold not
The left from right, but work the same.

When force of outside circumstance
Hurls outrage on the household shrine,
Kálù knows, all-seeing sky;
Àlà knows, wise earth divine.

These gods are not the sort to pardon
Even unintended revolt—
A lucky few snatch time to cleanse
Before blast of the thunderbolt.

Umune and Ụ̀mụ̀ ńné serve
Where history leaves refugees
(As I met life The Queen
Had much to answer from her colonies.)

They oversaw Mum's sixteen days
Of pampering when I was born—
News out to Cairo over wires
Which later signaled time to mourn.

My name truly belonged to me
At close of that post-birthing rite.
Úchèńnà is the father's will—
My own never outran his fight.

Ụ̀mụ̀ ńné are my mother's blood
(Umon gives them a different name):
Their hand versus Dad's act hold not
The left from right, but work the same.

That river is my destiny
Whose current is maternal grace,
Dad had to row his way ahead,
To scout out fertile living space.

The parents never tried to raise me
Hostage to their sacrifice,
But first-born nature urges on:
Meet their ambition at its price!

The thunder hails me ọ́párá:
"Ụ̀mụ̀nakanù, of that ilk!"
I surge out to some future on
The undertow in mother's milk.

Future is a frame of being
Only fortune can endow;
Those crafty shunts, my parent lines,
Collapse potential into now.

Umune, animate my days,
A healing palm on every flaw;
Àlà and Kálù, grant my works
The suasion of your great ọ̀fọ́.

Those sixteen days long past, it's now
My turn to heed dear mother's claim;
Ancestors, give me strength to earn
Her labors, and my father's name.

MANGO FLESH

I'd also forgotten—what crackling recall!—
The many shades of mango flesh,
The many shapings of mango flesh,
The many flavors of mango flesh,
The many textures of mango flesh,
The tumescences of varied fruit,
Sacred arrays upon seasonal trays,
Indiscreet colors ablush, all orange,
Formulae told at the tongue, all sweet.
Come like a mist the recollections
Of fluid sipped through a knife-slit hole,
Of opulent cubist self-serve bowl,
Of white-fibered stone with its cleave-to pulp,
The feed over seed of drupe occult.
In slurping up saffron from mango-ripe dawn,
I resound on the chord of my birthing song.

COLOSSUS

The man is through his left foot by tether of root tendrils,
By live axon leads plugged in sedimentary electrodes;
The circuit has the nerve to up his brain stem what he creates
And observes, to lightning catalyze and react and explode
When his kerosene blood meets sparked antennae atop his head.
It is eons downwards through this what used to be sea,
Adrip through coarse layers, adrip through fine, slow shift
    to bedrock.
A man must stand somewhere so that his surest self may be.

The man is through his right foot the utter old growth mangrove.
Chí ya di na m̀bá; that's where his hunger forever remains,
No matter how many days of mealtime he dines elsewhere.
His body heat derives from old radicals coursing his veins.
They'll stretch his roots out into space, his down the line offspring;
He must leave them sufficiency in charged fuel cells, he and
    his Chí,
At worldwide crossroads, at crotch that joins his leggy tree
    trunks—
A man must stand somewhere so that his surest self may be.

ỤMỤ̀ DÍ ỤZỤ́ (SMITH'S POSTERITY)

Sahel vulture even from his untrue height
Has learned better than to pause in flight above
Díké, he who can still make a true rifle shot
While hop-scotching minor markets, plying the rough
Road with strung cornelian on cord to trade.
That same road taken by middle peoples
Long ago scratched off from all reckoning,
Held only in memory of vultures and eagles.
They left Egypt, Meroe and Khartoum
Through high Sudan to proper forest Afara
Where they knocked over elephants and screamed
Mountain apes away, shaking off Sahara
To clear themselves the gods' own prize in farmland.
They soaked up the big water into their veins
To settle as earthen salt while fresh
Distillate wreathed their world in rains.

It's all for ivory, gold, copper ore,
Blackwood and nitrous soils that these leopard feet
Settled with smelting science so far from Nubia.
Thus bronze into high art rises on smithy heat,
For lost wax pieces that grace the Upper Nile
Over Chad Basin trade routes, borne on swift songs
That rings sand souks with Niger's un-Asian tongues.
The scorch-tempered vendors are paragons
In make-sway over bronze—tough hands, tough heads.

There you must follow, child; your blood-earned degree
Is your new passport back along ancestral lines.
We mete out according to ingenuity
Provisions for your chosen sojourn elsewhere;

For why shall we not wander now we have
This entire world as commonwealth to share.

Dí ụzụ, master smith, throttles every loop.
He enslaves the monkey, first cutting its tail.
He waits, beating practice time on drums,
The wax drain rhythm; waits for bronze to scale
The mold and sprue. He waits while dí ṅkà
Imposes humane notions on the wax.
Then dí ụzụ snatches back the work
Towards cool matter and unhumoring facts.
True, those far-off buyers like their ákụ́lụ́-ákụ́lụ́
But locals on the other hand had better
Take pride in rude shards. Fine plates are for export.
All Ìgbò customs station the debtor
Bottommost, so we come to hold temptation
To extravagance above all evil.
No time nor place for kings, nor for
Royal pretense in craft. We ply the needful.

Even díbịà with his strange tongues and herbs,
With more gods holding out their paws than clan
Members on title feast day, even díbịà
May not intrude beyond what the work plan
Outlines. From what dí ụzụ in his long tenure
Has seen, the one true god is a well-schooled,
Ruthlessly honest eye. The great story goes
That Chúkwú first set man above the world-pool,
On the only high enough land, an anthill,
From which narrow base Chúkwú's great adepts
Dried the shallows with flame blown by their bellows.
The master maker is the world's princeps.

This double bag of mortal breath that suits
Makings of some assured divinity
Is not Ìgbò alone. For Triple Brighid's
Dearest Erie the hero trinity
Are blacksmith, silversmith and carpenter.
They follow her in hospitality,
In leechcraft; their fabled acts attract the sidhe,
Bonding the maker with magic and poetry.

Sing-song Dí ákúkó carries a wineskin
Of praise for dí ụzụ , playing at useful
Misdirection to protect the valued trade-craft
From competing schemers. The truthful
Scene sees díbị̀à bless the magnetite, fine straw,
Hardwood coals and—most of all—kiln clay
Of termitarium, sacred source which, díbị̀à
Avers, lines every spirit passageway
To our world. Let others divine the clan
Next generation's strength from their bellows draft,
Or seek curse antidotes in slack water.
Dí ụzụ takes of such things cursory note;
Minding that his mainstay blessing is clean craft.

From untrue height of the wing-wright's triumph,
Over Sahel, from Lagos to Cairo,
A young man whose name claims him for the farm,
Not ụzụ, nevertheless takes his narrow
Post-war chance at engineering prestige.
He'd scarcely even heard of metallurgy,
Yet the old genius for materials found
His roving spirit willing. From that emerging
Field the new family line payed out digital,
Semiconductors upon his oxide
Start, and ceramics, all after metal, all bound
In cicatrice of myth fiercely denied.

The driven zebu watch vulture above,
Who scries even higher to the airplane:
There sits Díké, expanding his approach
To markets, tuning the wave of his brain
Away from colonial superstitions,
Which were given in place of ancestral lore.
All new roads challenging his ingenuity
Must take a proper Afara detour
Through unique heritage of master makers.
Let elephants and mountain apes return
With all creatures in their paleolithic place.
Díké must move on to his life's work: to learn
Where next and with what skill to lead his world,
His ever-growing sphere of commonwealth,
Above the vulture and airplane, there is rock
In space for the master maker to smelt.
There are markets to establish at Lagrange.
Dí ụ̀zụ́ takes his smithy and fire, swift songs,
Carpentry and healing over the moon,
That stars ring rough with Niger basin tongues.

ELECTRON MICROSCOPY

Materials engineering hardened in the heat of the space race, studying the fine properties of materials used in all parts of spacecraft, from outer hull and heat shields to high performance engine cores, making all the difference between success and failure in that harsh environment. The electron microscope became an important tool for materials engineers soon after its invention, allowing them to examine important crystalline details at the atomic level. A certain Nigerian student at Case Western Reserve University, while completing his Mat. Eng. Ph.D. under Dr. T. E. Mitchell, performed pioneering electron microscopy work in this area, authoring numerous papers before eventually returning to Nigeria to help found several university Engineering departments.

I

What was he doing those nights on the battered
Murals of my primordial memories?
That shell mystery has never really mattered.

I place him in his still laboratories,
Charting textures where electrons scattered,
For translation into material stories.

Lightning over my chopped seas of recall
Gives spectral, snap life to promontories:
Grey impressions or landed fact? I don't trawl

Those waters on purpose; I dare not risk
The monsters' reveal in nets at landfall,
What might be reanimated by such brisk

Electron beams on my mind's substrate,
Scoring my childhood by asterisk.
That hint of eruption in estate—

A hopeless search for Mother; a separate scene
Watching an abstract fuel station conflagrate,
In two-storey flames, blent into a dream

Of Mount Megiddo, heaving me from bed
To find our flat empty. No point in the scream,
Small boy, turn on the lights and read instead.

II
Oh how the electron beam could more
Than measure or illume; it could impose
Design, manipulate, brain-fruit of Bohr,

Who, in the books I lugged from the library,
Filled out Rutherford's flat models, wherefore
The brace rod and ping-pong ball tracery

About my father's desk, and, from the outlook
Under halls wheezing with machinery,
The shadow relief photos in his logbook.

Walking home each day he'd scour thrift shops,
Wells and Verne for intellectual hook,
Then encyclopædia volumes set as backstops.

It was grandfather's impulse struck anew
My family's ambitious eye to mountaintops,
Relentless, driving home: Ụ́mụ̀nakanù.

Dad knew his doom: no matter what his talents
The world would mark him illustre inconnu
While in Nigeria those who raked in rents

Would take the headlines; but perhaps his sons
Could be thrust up beyond their precedents,
Supply our name with laurels, and with funds.

III

Stress patterns in oxidized silicates,
Sintered granules with their locking jaws
And latticework of crystal delicates:

In these habitats he hunted flaws
Which served for an abundance of papers;
Sometimes this hunt would take him past his pause,

As if the prepping chemical vapors
Blurred his sense of place and even hour;
Perhaps we seemed to him as lit by tapers,

Removed from his great instrument's power.
But what ambitious materials engineer
Would let their sample drop before they scoured

Its every feature for a bulge or tear?
And though the human element's a jinx,
He was quite well equipped to persevere:

He'd been to Luxor to confront the Sphinx
So he'd learned his way around a riddle.
Presented with his own domestic links,

It was a binary search, sliced at the middle,
Of entrails dry of publishable findings,
Leading into sore temptation to fiddle.

IV

The gash in Dad's career came when he set
The focal point along the Niger's east
Where his caliber of research was as yet

Science fiction. Lecturing seemed good enough
Until he found industry under threat
From quick-rich frenzy in crude; finding it tough

To inspire students with space shuttle
Ambitions; he had to seize them by their scruff,
Exhibiting Bini Lost Wax rebuttal

To their lazy equating of high tech
With the West. Too soon, Dad had to scuttle
Even that modest craft, quit the wreck;

Back to NASA and the tunnel microscope,
To niece and nephew echoes from his priestly beck,
Throwing matched talent after the same skied hope:

My glassworks engineer adept, cousin Brian,
And Ubu, Doctor of silicated stope,
Whose tragic death still haunts our family line.

Born in scrutiny of Dad's scanning tip
Shall I bear truth in the clan's ensign,
Bear out his quantized quest of Serendip?

WHY SHOULD I MURMUR?

Know what disease prowls just to the right blind of clear sight,
Pack of reinforced jaws.
Know I only keep it away by burning this candlewick-top plasma,
Body of heat, no matched security light.
No light to read from; I won't bother to squint over what
My father has already told me.
He gets the needle directly into the eye from the lab coats
    fortnightly.
This he casually describes.
The man entirely becomes the lectern, in front of a class so much
    of his life,
So when he admits trouble sleeping,
It sounds like the treatise on eigenvectors he gave me in fifth
    form,
An uncoordinate space
Distorted by episodes of breath in rag-patterning, dithered in
    the knots,
Kom-kom against shallow ribs,
He has close study on each valve's art in prolapse,
Approaching asymptote of snap collapse,
One beat
Before the electrified jacket outside,
One beat
Before the electrified lozenge within,
Right at the heart of him.

Know I've earned my marks because I've never known a doctor
Not to frown at my heartbeat
Between their looped drum, across the stethoscope that makes
    calipers

Across the odd measure of me,
They are wide pupils to glance, astonished, at their sphygmomano.

I have seen kin faces on the news,
I have seen kin faces flash in youth and relative youth
While phone calls from relatives slugged their grief
And shock into my half-leaden ear.
These walkers of my tribe reach with muscling, surly vigor,
Such dense mettle, indeed bones of a metal that attracts the
Sudden course of lightning to ground state.

My share is hypertension squared,
Blue bulge blood from both parents,
Sire and distaff, royal allowance of three pills per day.
They raised me to live in the great state of despite,
And since I am the son, why should I fear, why should I murmur?

If the squeeze fleeces me for an organ,
I may wait too long to know;
My blood's murmuring hides its own secrets too well,
Its wins and wounds at the outpost.
I'm left the brazier lit at father's warning,
Carefully tended engine with its Carnot cycles—
Fasting and athletics on either flank of indulgence.

My blood's miles murmur ancestral code,
Words long lost to me, words I cannot tell.
My blood's miles forecast aortal surge,
Each drop, each mote in ever more certainty.
There is more than the moon's tide over lively waters
Where some of us made infamous landing.
I am by outer and inner life always on the edge
Of impossibly big ṁmírí,
A river so wide its far bank is gossip of prophets.
Even the village stream has ripples to tickle the bush at its edge;

The Niger's waves sashay for the keen-eyed;
And no one fails to notice breakers at South Bonny beach;
The sake of my breath makes swell high overhead.
But why should I murmur against the surf?
However the crested billows threaten,
Love slumbers under their foamy old frown,
Where there! just there! rolls somewhat of my father in them.

AT THE UNIVERSITY OF PORT HARCOURT
TEACHING HOSPITAL

Through fly-trap filaments, blurred gum of an opening eye—
Five heads over me. According to wall and ceiling cracks,
All of us floating in mute vacuum of a white vault.

I think I remember a typical morning, relaxed,
With ♪*Radio Rivers 2...*♭ over the Peugeot speakers.
I'd turned from Choba traffic into gbom-gbom of East-West Road;
The corner hawkers jogged after me a few meters,
Never minding the morning rain on their head-borne loads.

Somewhere more in time than place—fog mounts—
Cap of my skull has slipped over my eyes.
A voice cuts through my struggle with recall,
One solidly sensed thing in all the haze.

Do you know your name? Pain.
Do you know where you are? Pain.
Do you know what happened? Pain.

At once the heads in my view were blistered by greater light—
Magnesium fuse. Each breath pulled a barbed, white-hot line
    to draw me
From smoulder of counterfeit sleep towards broad flame of day
    sight.

The dark behind so deep, this flood so utterly searing,
I wondered: could my memory of driving through rain have swum
    through
Intervening years? I thrashed again, this time with sense of time.
That same voice knew to say "ǹdó" to slow my ungoverned spin,

So one or both of us were Ìgbò, one clue of whatever
As I scried my own traces through the mountain summit mist.
It made sense I did not know where I was going next,
But why could I perceive nothing besides some tattered gist
Of all my life before, no more than brief chinks showing
Lichenous rock and hermit grass of living moments?
If these, the brown-faced in white shifts are magistrates
Of after-death's assizes, how shall I swear, deponent,
With so little gathered to show from my own journey?

Ñdó. Suffri-suffri. oh!

The voice again, one of two solid, experienced poles,
The other, **pain**, residing fireanthill under my lungs.
Glowing beyond both, and sometimes slipping into my reach,
A surprising benevolence. Could I count cherubs
Dancing on my belly's bed of nettles? Could I seize one,
Reverse its bumblebee flight back into full understanding,
Of my life were it not over; of the cosmos, were it?
I felt my inertial frame slow down, some sort of landing.
Whatever craft this was turned its light shield to the star.
I could now see passing rows of beds. The bolus of pain
Turned bolide and swallowed me, and by the time it faded
I was in a bed of my own, a bit more in my own brain.

I am Doctor Adotey. These are my students.

A new voice; this was increasingly like earthly existence,
But something in my veins still had me ballooned aloft.

Ọ dị ḿmá

First voice, and this time coinciding with a body.
I do feel that; thanks; you've taken my hand, Medicine Mr. Man.
Why can I not quite hold it up myself? That is, I think,

Where you would find my pulse were I where I think I am,
But go ahead and squeeze anyway; please do squeeze.
Perhaps you can pump out of it the nebulous wildcard
Of my perceptions, leaving me assurance that I live,
Or perhaps assurance that not living needn't be so hard.

OGBÚNÀBÀLÌ AND HYPNOS, 1949

Ogbúnàbàlì, god of death at still night
Completed his journey from the deep delta
Under the city's seven gold-flung hills.
Here was a complex of zinc-roofed shelter,
A sign: Ibadan College Hospital.

To the initiated eye here also rose
A cave mouth of roots wormed from Mokola hill,
Trimmed with broken marble. Here lounged Hypnos,
Fanning himself with a titan peacock quill
Until Ogbú's rasping voice held him.

You returned with our sons from your white tribelands
With medicine that's neither sleep nor death,
That moulders in between. You would come
To my delta realm next; The urgent breath
Of my brother Ikú peals this alarm.

You salt Ikú's mouth with forbidden yam flour
When he comes to his farm for rightful crop.
Àgbìgbò, coffin maker now squats with you.
You should dread the coffin on your rooftop
Where he placed it. Leave us be, and our world.

Hypnos shifted on his dank clay couch and spoke:
You end your long trek by accusing the wrong
Party; Not long ago my own Lethe
Was abstracted away. They do grow strong,
Our charges. Every god becomes their victim.

Ogbúnàbàlì smells truth like forest rain.
These humans are climate, shifting the plots
Of divine farms. But they can yet no more steal
His cutlass than relieve the sun of its spots.
Ikú still swings his cudgel to doom's effect.

Hypnos rose and led Ogbú on a ward tour
One patient swooned to the masked doctor's blade,
The specter of yam flour sprinkled on his eyes,
The Lethe ghost-lined into his veins
By a gloved hand attentive to his pulse.

The tour over, Hypnos produced kolanut.
Is this fruit not the local seal of bonds,
And so where you come from as well? Let us break
Into its bitterness, as man breaks with rods
Of invention all old nuances of gods.

MYSTERIES OF HARVEST: HOME

Bounty by palm,
Its wine-tap bole,
Its kernel oil
For new roast yam;

Surprise sweets trail
Of termite roast;
Earth on the nose—
Under giant snail;

Cashew for fruit
Then (careful!) seed,
The yard goat's meat
With ụgụ shoot;

All slow-pot stew,
My love for you.

TWO KITCHENS

I was alone, but my hand took on my mother's,
Hovering over the pot with a gestured command,
Smothering all thought inessential to the task,
All distractions from the essences I'd ranged:
Cinnamon, cardamom, and then, slither-charmed
From coriander, cumin and turmeric
I swelled to the stove, which sprang wormhole
To Chengdu, to Tehran, to Kabul and Lhasa,
And over the möbius loop to Lomé, Yaoundé and Calabar.
To fistfuls of waterleaf, ùtázì sprinklings,
Periwinkle with the waste ends sheared,
All royal spit-curl prominences,
And the languages that whirly-jigged that kitchen,
Umon, Efik, Ìgbò, English,
Scolding, praise, intrigue, the neighbor's business,
Indeed the neighbor's rat-skulled dog...
One sudden spark shunted all that distance
To light the burner, snapping me to the present,
Checking my shirt for scorch marks
(how long had I stood in fugue with the gas on?)
My burnt fingertip and singe-haired nose
Led me back to my duty where a spiced lamb dish
Awaited its anointed assembly.

RUN IT!

Run it this way, Hammurabi.   Run it this way, Liebnitz.
It's mine!   It's mine!

Run it this way, Galenus.   Run it this way, Al Kwarizmi
It's mine!   It's mine!

Run to me waters, to marshal of your springs,
Run softly, sweet rivers, listen to my song,
Listen as they snore, as I kill them softly,
Swell to my staff, to my sea where you belong.

Run to me whatever kennings I desire;
Find me where potential guides your swift flow;
Where I beat this deep valley with my bare feet,
Where I've stamped out all the bases: need to know.

Run your languages this way; I want all your words
With their secrets, picklocks to your treasure chest;
Indic and European my usurper stock talk—
Bastard children of theirs ring out at my behest.

Run to me with your Moses in a basket,
Phoenician heliotrope from your shellfish shoals;
Phoenix sings the blues born again in your alphabets,
Got your convert philosophers hooked by their souls.

Run from this valley when my song excites you;
Watch the tentative tyrant army advance;
Slow! They're too slow! I've mined the dry bed;
Rush back to drown them at signal of my dance.

Run your sciences this way, I want your redrum natura
All these worlds are mine, *including* Europa;
Run those numbers, I'm here to collect,
Cornu in hand for swag bag of your copia.

Run me your logic of prank propositions,
Nine spheres of your seven loaf and fish tales;
I'll take Ibn Rushd over your Uni Parisians—
Stigmata dogmata flush up your high swales.

Run this way wet dendrites of world-nerve,
Run Tiber, Alphaeus and Xanthos-Skamander;
Even hell and heaven are mine to explore
River-charmed skin plays sylph and salamander.

Run your schools by me, I'll take the library,
I'll take the bursary too, and the work without wage;
Turn over your log tables, flasks and retorts,
I'll have telescope and micrometer screw gauge.

Run your machines for my careful inspection,
I might use some earthworks, a handful of hand tools,
You can keep all that hydroengineering, though,
Save me, great ladies from overreach of fools.

Run your arts this way, pictures, stories and songs,
I've built the museum, time to set up display;
Peace unto you in your alien ritual
I'm far too catholic for auto da fé.

Run chart-smart in my terra incognita
I'll offer you secrets your children ignored;
My ancestral mysteries are watershed gems—
It's bounty to share, take heaps from the hoard.

Run to a face they're shy to recognize:
Not looking Italian, Semitic or Greek,
Yet I inherit; pragmatic exchange:
I pay up indulgence their testaments seek.

Run rivers of Babylon—Tigris, Euphrates,
Draw me welled tears from their mountains of pride;
Don't fear for your courses, I'll nurture your flocks,
They'll blend our traditions and witness them wide.

Run it this way, Mozart.   Run it this way, Petrarca.
It's mine!   It's mine!

Run it this way,   Run it this way, Sappho.
Schopenhauer. It's mine!   It's mine!

2/ OJUKWU

A SIXTEEN FOR COL. OJUKWU

To the tune of Ice Cube - Amerikkka's Most Wanted [The Bomb Squad, with love to a multitude of sample sources]

Leader of Biafra, and outstanding military pioneer for Nigeria before that.

If Zik was MLK, who vexed like Malcolm x,
Never letting the feds take all his people's heads.
Emeka's father had the riches, but he broke against his wishes
To ride his own train to be the pride of the militias.
He stood officious in opposing the Nzeogwu coup,
Didn't go through, he joined the gunner governor crew.
The rainy season's flood was blood, so the Colonel understood
To end the massacres, his people needed nationhood
Knew human nature is base, wouldn't embrace for the good.
Plus the generals were all belting out for the pedestal.
They tried in Aburi to bury the hatchet fully
But he couldn't yank the brick from the fist of the bully
So Biafra was born, a flag, and anthem and much more
The sun rose red in the east into the rage of a storm
The man was brave and stubborn, yet all the blaze was southern
But though we paid in burns, we made the fight on our own terms.

ÒZÒGBÚ-ÒZÒGBÚ

Thunder can break—Earth, bind me fast—
Obduracy, the disease of elephants.

—Christopher Okigbo

Speak ényì and enter.
Speak friend and enter?
Speak ényì and enter.
Speak ényí and enter?
Speak elephant, friend of all entrances,
All openings; nothing dare block your way.
Nothing dare refrain from giving you chance.
Your way is the downhill road of rumor.
Your might makes instant right of way rule.
Speak friend, so bush leaf repeated rumor
Speeds you on your way back to our, your town.

But the English writ, Latiny squiggle,
Makes in Ìgbò quibbles,
Fiddles with impossibilities,
Scatters sense indeed. No one can yoke
Elephant. Even his friend can't stop him.

Ényímbà Ényí (Òzògbú)
Ényímbà (Òzògbú-Òzògbú)
Ényímbà Ényí (Òzògbú)
Ényímbà (Òzògbú-Òzògbú)

Òzògbú-Òmánwú!

Igboland night dresses its truth in terror,
Fractal terror insistent at every scale,
If you haven't been inoculated.
Malaria and its old friends awaited
Even the first masters at gunboat arms;
The hatter syndrome, mercurial madness,
Claimed their later surrogates and proxies,
Sarzent tumbled upon Black Night! Black Night!
Mistah Kurtz dead from horror! The Horror!
Oh that's Agwu Nsi swinging poisoned
Frangipane out of the hot brass censer
He seized from a catholic missionary.
Here even the sun's own disinfectant
Failed with its setting. Don't cry for that age.
We are the soil's issue. We still full ground.
While we're still inoculated that age
Survives. Are we still inoculated?
Sing out those songs. Let's be sure. Sing right out!
Don't let choirmaster's head nod to the night.
Don't let the lead into the dancer's feet.
Don't let the lurgy into chorus lungs.

Let Ìgbò night songs swell our legs to beat;
Leap up with calves only jí produces
Elephant muscle move! Stomp it down! Sing!

Ényíḿbà Ényí (Ǹzǫ̀gbú)
Ényíḿbà (Ǹzǫ̀gbú-Ǹzǫ̀gbú)
Ényíḿbà Ényí (Ǹzǫ̀gbú)
Ényíḿbà (Ǹzǫ̀gbú-Ǹzǫ̀gbú)

Ǹzǫ̀gbú-Nwókè!

Òbí Kérérénkè	*Òbí!*
Kérérénkè	*Òbí!*
Nwókè máa mmà	*Òbí!*
Nwókè di n'Army;	*Òbí!*

And just so, at Owèrrè, at Uli,
Nsukka *kwanu*, numbed and outnumbered,
Gung-ho but well outgunned. Egyptians buzzed,
Vultures overhead, their droppings terror,
Strafing our hamlets, bombing our òbís
(*Òbí Kérérénkè, Òbí! Gbáa-la ájí na ámù*)
Goodwill came from Nyerere, and then help
From Israel, but alas not many more.
Starving, we had only goat-fodder leaves
Chewed to strains of songs promising us
Indomitability.   *Ojukwu ka anyi ga e soo.*
We had the masterclap of Ógbúnígwè,
The westward counter-offensive of Banjo
And Ifeajuna, burned out at Ore,
Ojukwu the savior didn't even
Ascend Gowon's well-prepared rebel cross.
Onwuatuegwu could not assure victory,
Great as he was, true to his name as he was.
Nor Okigbo nor Achebe could write
A victory. No one could assure victory,
Not even elephant (poachers were too many),
Until time came, time for the elephant.

Ényímbà Ényí (Ñzògbú)
Ényímbà (Ñzògbú-Ñzògbú)
Ényímbà Ényí (Ñzògbú)
Ényímbà (Ñzògbú-Ñzògbú)

Ñzògbú-Nwányí!

Aba Commission looked into the eyes
Of nwányị ndi Ìgbò and blinked astonishment.
Ndi Baikie had adapted the science of regency
From ancient Rome and here was a new concept.
What sort of thing this feminarum fasces?
Our mothers fell in front of the warrant courts,
Mown down by Lewis gun, nude from protest.
Their children's victory was their own, their will.
Aba Commission could not understand.
They'd stamped trade with ụmụ̀ nwókè, thrust up
Hamlet chiefs on any convenient claim,
Patronized the watching Ìgbò matron,
Ényì, it was. Friend. So from where came this
Elephant? These blasted Igbos and their
Crazy language! What Ndi Baikie couldn't
Quite make out from assumption was the cleft
Of this new world, symbolized by two words
Entirely separate in dimensions
Well beyond them. When the commissioners'
Successors conceded independence
To these women's children, they'd learned something.
They gave it up without a shot. No fight.
They clumped together quarrelsome neighbors
With starchy institutions, took their leave
And kept a skance-eyed watch. Did they not know
A fight would come? There was always a fight
Coming. With or without the warrant courts
A fight was coming, coming, always coming.

Ényímbà Ényí (Ǹzọ̀gbú)
Ényímbà (Ǹzọ̀gbú-Ǹzọ̀gbú)
Ényímbà Ényí (Ǹzọ̀gbú)
Ényímbà (Ǹzọ̀gbú-Ǹzọ̀gbú)

Ǹzọ̀gbú-Ényí!

Britain and all Europe, the USA
And Canada, the booming gulf and Asia;
Professionals, journeymen and crooks,
We had the bush, now we'll have the world,
Softly softly now, we've no truck with crowns
Our way is to punch through the soft center
Of marketplaces, those we understand.
Ọwụ́ ótú ányí na-e mèé; Òbí!
But before long came Gbuum! They blew
Outwards, the brown, dehiscent pods
Gbem! Division. Gbam! Diaspora.

WHATEVER happened to the elephant?

Age old rain forest, impenetrable
(Ónyé íjè, are you still inoculated?)
Impenetrable even to Baikies
Gave way to cocoa in rashed regiments,
To oil palm in sprawling monoculture.
The tetrarch of the jungle lost his ground
(Elephants done commot; them no full ground)
Poachers spotted them thanks to mile-long
Gaps along rubber tap plantation rows.
Now we're lucky to encounter the rare few:
Omo-Shasha, Oluwa, North Cross River,
Or northward, Kamuku or Yankari,
Sic transit Loxodonta Cyclotis.
Tùfíákwà! Ọwụ́ árụ́rụ́ àlà.
Who are we, the people, home or worldwide?
What are we without the people's elephant?

Ényíḿbà Ényí (Ǹzọ̀gbú)
Ényíḿbà (Ǹzọ̀gbú-Ǹzọ̀gbú)
Ényíḿbà Ényí (Ǹzọ̀gbú)
Ényíḿbà (Ǹzọ̀gbú-Ǹzọ̀gbú)

Friend, Colonel of all great entrances,
All great movements, not least those of people,
Lead the way back. Nothing dare block your way.
Nothing dare refrain from giving you chance.
Your way is the downhill road of rumor.
Your might makes instant right of way rule.
Speak friend, so bush-leaf repeated rumor
Speeds you on your way back to our, your town.

Ényímbà Ényí (Ǹzọ̀gbú)
Ényímbà (Ǹzọ̀gbú-Ǹzọ̀gbú)
Ényímbà Ényí (Ǹzọ̀gbú)
Ényímbà (Ǹzọ̀gbú-Ǹzọ̀gbú)

RAVENANT

How rather rich of us to intimate,
In wild-eyed tales by the fireplace, that ghosts
Are vagabond victims necklaced in hunger,
Reaching out fleshless hands to beseech us
For food purchased at crossroads market booths,
Between-world fare. The clan dines lushly the day
A child slams the gate against inchoate wilds
To take on evidence of a staying name;
We say his former friends stretch see-through fingers
To steal ube, okpa and ogbono soup
From our long tables, and with a weighty nod:
Good trade to jog off such plague customers.
At harvest feasts enough is served for portion
Pledged to ancestors, and though we don't mention,
To pest spirits as well. We tell tales of skull
Creatures known to kidnap good cooking wives,
Gleeful details—their cursed-open hinges—
As if such were the common theft of meat
Sliced from ample racks at the abattoir;
We grow weed of idle rumors at weddings,
Local god galas, potlatch after seasons
In profit; we grow weed where it most thickly
Chokes the plots—among drawn, mourning faces.
Whether it was in time or in tragedy
We see off one of our own, whether the feast
Will break out in joy or smolder in hushed tones,
We usher the dead before the living
Procession along generous rows of yam
And crocks of stocked palm oil, as if to serve
As ironical witnesses in public
Ceremony against any potential
Claim of poisoning by the plenty merchants.

Those who travel east come back crying:
Look now! Those people even talk of pretas
Disturbing everybody for something
To consume. At this they suck their teeth
Towards the supposed realm of hungry wraiths.
Those who journey west, to oyinbo say:
See! This their kind of skull-bone Halloween, sef!
So so cut-up pumpkins and skeleton sweets!
That ghosts return upon us to be fed
Is worldwide chauvinism; only human
To take our fret over mysteries of harvest,
Our memories of misery in famine
For some sort of lex cosmologica.
And Christians, sef, this their cannibal wafer,
Their vampire wine. This mass be like say man-mess.
Is it not more likely that specter babies
Crave a father's compound in which a mother's arms?
That ancients of our ilk feed on memory
Which reheats them to their own of this life?
But such is not the substance of bargain,
Which is how we come to understand the world.

When their bush irrupts into our compounds,
Phantasms must slot their zero time into
Our mornings, nights and years. Their hyperspace
Must be uncrumpled into our metrics.
The daemonic is at once on top of us
And at a remove askew and infinite;
What passes in their way for workings of mind
Appears to us as food, and we are each meal,
And no less with each physiological pang
Plucking at visceral strings upon the song
That plays its register throughout the cosmos.
Needs only hum its overture as you station

Yourself at any crossroads to begin
An honest commerce with the numinous.

Take one psychotropic hero who on his way
Back from the Town of Deads encounters the most
Fearful of all his bush and road perils,
The hungry-hungry-hungry. In taking
This noise literally he wobbles off guard
And soon finds his wife and loads, and then himself
Entrapped in the entity's deadly vacuum.
He has the magical resource to slash
Their way out to safety, but not all shall have.

The use of food shall not exceed the straight
Masonry of foundation under ribs.
What shadows disturb us while we're alone,
What shadows invite themselves to gatherings
Are cunning negotiators. They'll trade
In terms of meal and useless ectoplasm,
And put paid to our human grace in dealing.

Look for no currency in old fireplace rumors;
Insist on discipline to address all things,
Even death itself, in terms of the living.
Fufu lumps are not consumed without soup
But you don't buy the gari at the same stall
As egusi, okro or waterleaf.
You must learn the whole marketplace, ényì,
By following the chef rather than the priest.

MYSTERIES OF HARVEST II

Renew, Ahiajioku, our once pursuit
Of leg-long yam thatched into barns to mark
Well-honored compounds, goddess-blest tasked with stark
Display, bounty for faith in toil and fruit,
For sweat miracles blooded on matchet blades
As starch-powdered sap, white flesh, grey rind,
And green of close-crop úgú set for soup sign,
Spread at New Yam fêtes, our triumphal parades.

Till Christians came—Ijaw and Aro thrust
Through Abiriba, through Ohafia that cult
Of chains and blood. Thus Àlà in her rage
Brought blight to yam where blighted wars were waged;
Cassava reigns, bastard lord, shrunken result
From loam corrupted into red, red dust.

IKOT ABASI MBONG

Once the taxi bus exhaust fumes separated us
From welter of the motor park, the green rushed right through,
Tinting our glances and vocabularies. She'd already known
This transition—here was her posting—she meant this view
For my convalescent, supposed poet eyes. The deep delta,
Niger rune ruffled a-sudden by its own masquerade
In sharded mirror skin, thus slivered into brown tendrils,
Each purling to its ancient hamlets milk of some lost trade,
Each swelling drink straws to unslakable mangrove thirst;
Only metallic cackle of the gas flares could jog the spell.

Here was paradise with a trocar in its neck and traces
Of infection painting its fainted rose, but who was to tell?
Time swallowed up those quarters, sparing but drops of memory—
A soup cooked with palm oil, blendspice, waterleaf, bitterleaf
And egusi from the local junction's fresh goods market.
We traded gist of history while walking aperitif,
University types jawing out yarns of juju King Jaja.
The food had an overpowering aftertaste of ruin,
Inedible. A day's hair growth of poison signalled
Just enough on the nose to announce the tongue's undoing.
She admitted that prior to my coming she'd been eating
Mostly packaged fare, not normally to the health,
With little thought as to why.

                    Time swallowed up those quarters
But I remember songs of the delta's primordial wealth,
Songs that would snatch me up nights from tangle among
    her limbs

To rove out on the porch clap-stamping out and writing down.
My kerosene lamp turned, when pencil touched paper, a gas flare
Spreading yellow sick-leaf over green, over fountainhead brown.

FISH EYED JONAHS

Best Laid Schemes of Fish or Men

1651

This spicefish fanning its gills to sniff freedom
Of Biafara Bight can thank hardwood hulls
That loaf along above, weird new species
That's appeared to distract the muscled men
Whose tichier boats, walls of net, and vise arms
Were once proliferating bane of the school.

The fish give their design to french parasols
The fish skim sandbars where dead hands clutch cowries;
Iridescence of fish scales shingles
A trove of scrap tins and silvers buffed
And shape-sheared into brooches, badges and crowns—
Factitious bait come inward as ballast.

Fish cousins further out from Annobón
Dodge a rain of manillas under storms
When Ówú Ḿmírí shrieks her sudden squalls
When rage of alien deities builds up a blaze
From kindling wrath of homeland counterparts
When Ndem flips a giant fin below waves,
She-Jove splintering galleons just short of Thebes.

At times even with no tempest above
Comes hail of black skin rippling rivulets
Of muscle against chains and shacklebolts,
Comes hail of limp forms in slough of sickness
Comes fleshly hail, hunks within red billows

Where squid and shark squads meet unfathomable
Bodyfall as it perturbs the surface.

On broom of currents sweeps scent of these portents
Towards coastal fish who wonder at such signs;
How should they know it shall end in poisoned seas,
This play of prospectors and their cunning plans:
Act one: Turn hounds of murder loose upriver.
Act two: Tutor toughs to be fishers of men.
Act three: seize the New World for fresh fish market.
Now stand back on the strand to reap the catch.
Your manillas will buy you run of the coast;
Your cowries will penetrate the forests
Of lost wax where base metal has no lure.

Send in your thieves under sigil of Ichthys
To debate retainers of masquerades
To debate prelates of rain forest gods
To make up kings where once the people found
A fish story in such royal claims.
Send them in to take on the self spirits
Who serve as die of each newborn person
Who stamp the life but cast its lots afresh.
You may ball these all together and call them
Fetishes, totems, idols, man engaged
In making of gods. You may claim your own god
Is one, the singular maker of men,
The singular fisherman whose juju
Sweeps men and women into baleen net
Of wooden whales in sail across the waters.

1894

Send in your thieves on bicycles, arms full
Of writs and bibles, armaments on standby.
Should your creed not take of its own cold charm,
Send in shock troops, rockets, Lewis guns;
Nothing multiplies the fish symbol flock
Quite like a good passage of massacres.

1961

A long pause, pandemonium on the shore,
And here's a new sort of trade in black gold,
Here's a new floating species, not the swordfish
Analogue of galleons, but the nightshade hold
Of leviathan, gorged on gallon and barrel
Of lethal obsidian milk of warmongers,
Of the world's pound of flesh by rotted blood,
Of toxic mojo sucked through trocar stuck
In ancient forest loams and deep sea floor.

1983

The fish schools at tide shoulders cannot dodge
This new fallout from trade lines over horizon.
Crude insistence of waste paints mangrove limbs,
Tars sands and films over gills in choke-out slick.
These dead fish swimming are still ostensibly
Free to roam the bight all their zombie lifespan—
Unto this generation muscled men
Have not resumed their old world pulling of nets,
Their more direct anti-fish terror; they race
Instead with motor racket over waves,
Some wearing hard hats, some wearing rifles,
To and from mid-ocean surface-scrapers.

On land they knock seaside muck from their boots
Outside bukaterias for roast croaker,
Outside churches with fish signs and motto boards
With dubious claims to offer loaves and fish
Aplenty for the seaside multitude.

2062

Only the fish who has become the catch
Observes from belly of the wicker trap
The excess swagger of another's fin flap.

A little boy of Bonny creek pedigree
Shrugs off the missal for the surf and ducks
To ask the bulge-eyed school their deep soothsay.
The fish has already refused to carry
The kelp sprig of warning unto his land,
So the boy comes too late, finding them clapped up,
Jonahs in a carbonic acid bath,
This frankenstein leviathan world of men.

ELEPHANT HEAD [ÍSÍ ÉNYÍ]

The people, marching, bend their knees like tree trunks
This is how often they've been left for broken
In certain wooded hollows lie unhallowed skulls
Mutilated—the tusks have been torn off for tokens.

True king of the jungle, four legged, does no sort
Of Hollywood wailing, of Hollywood swinging—
Almighty in weight but watch them butterfly float
Once provoked, their trunk turned off stun, set stinging.

There was once a head that rose through eddy currents
To batter slack boats with unschooled pilots
Now only oil slicks trouble the surface
And any bullet-headed fool calls themself pirate.

The river's regent never breathed through gills
While picking their teeth with a fallen tree limb
But take even a fish under alien waters
And watch liars convince them they cannot swim.

The people's trunk shook tree tops down for fruit,
Reached over the bank to pull up a drink
Where once the python was lord of the path
Now churches spring up—how the great go extinct.

Movement of the people was an ease for feeding
Movement of the people was a grave-making quake
Armies of poachers carved their ivory thrones
They shall yet be trampled to learn their mistake.

Some river people were taken by boat
Under gun and chain over high Atlantic.
Their blood sweat stolen, sold back by the cynics
As the latest wisdom in wealth mathematics.

The elephant's skull grows white under sunlight
Leaking through lumber camps and poisoned trees
The people's heads, replaced by machines,
Forget the blood-sweat that still flows overseas.

Rainforest elder, mahogany genius,
Now mostly on film, distant zoos and museums
Five continents have their own Wounded Knee
With gift shops on exiting the mausoleums.

The poachers taught Shakespeare; said: *Lend me your ears*
And proceeded to cut the ears off at the neck
Lost with their head is the people's history
How long shall this ruse keep the people in check?

Hippopotamus ears, then eyes and nostrils
Shall give no warning before they emerge
To smash some new boats, old river surprise;
Watch the people stomp anchor against the sea surge.

Flesh become machine shall once again be flesh
We, headless yet never forgetting, advance
Up from rivers to oceans of stars, watch the dark
Of our people's heads feel out the expanse.

OKOBI AND THE CRYING...

I

So what are you saying?
We are all cowards in this village?
    A chalk-man of cassava flesh
    Ignores the mighty leopard men of Amaraku
    And lays an iron path through our own yam plots
    Terrifying us with his blockhead beasts?

Éyéé! What has become of Amaraku
    in these short years I've been away;
        where are the stalwarts my father knew?
Now that my father is old and infirm
Can he do anything
    but watch
        his sons and brothers
            allow ghosts
                to appropriate
                    our family land...

What is that noise?

Eh? Take me to this iron path
And while my Okobi blood leaps through my veins
No beast or bastard shall cross our land!

II

Ah! There comes the pale man's gwon-gwoni nnama.
What racket it makes as it runs along.
But do we not say, oh Amaraku

That the troublesome child at play
　　is louder by far than the crouching hunter,
　　that the titled man never scampers in his own compound?
Come forth you noisy demon:
It is on the Okobi farm you shall stop...

What is that noise?

Ha, look! I haven't even touched the thing
And already it is wailing,
Some diseased elephant sneeze!
The iron beast is crying, oh!

Just wait until Okobi's hand
touches your insolent cheek.

There it cries again.
Here I stand, son of Okobi,
My sharpened matchet in my hand,
On your wood and iron path.
You have insulted Amaraku and now
On the Okobi farm you shall stop!...

RHEOTYPE

My voice out to you
Cold calling your presumptions,
Nothing in it
But my native contradictions.
I massive in my multitudes,
I round Mount Zion Zambian
And zig-zag-ur-rat-a-tat
Built up from that view;
I am Babel you screw up
Your ears to construe.
You heard of hand-me downs
To the continent
On ships from Euro-label-owned
Asian sweatshops,
As I've heard your handed-down
Africology, all huts and stour
With baby death's head highlights,
Set under with subtitles
Even when Nini brings it Quin's English.
(This dour documentary brought to you
By Soi-Disant productions.)
Didn't you just say "Bantustan?"
I got your grubby tongue-glut right here
Like the seven black candles
In your cack-handed kumbaya
Kwanzaa Black Friday display.

Sorry, I'm interrupting. Who am I then,
All high-street happening-now?
Who fit my jungle thighs
For your Jet spread boutique-cut fashion?

Oh you mistook me for Benetton:
Here's another beatnik bumbershoot
Easing on down by the rain-ditch rainbow façade!
I done bulged up your bell curve,
And you're going to need a Wangary Masai spear
For this scale in boil-lancing.
Don't gag on all that whitening fluid,
Hold the freeze-dried reflex.
Leave your mouth O for chaos, chaps,
Because some of us don't claim descent from Khufu.
Some of us have no time for African kings and queens
Because we've come through the milliard seed,
Through twelve republican generations.

Here I come, all that and less,
Vagabond lord of the long bond,
Middle-class perversion of marabout.
We've been two billion tear ducts
And I'm merely a blockage of one;
Call me your equation's fudge,
Veritable variable
Within my sealed specific.

Talk to me when you wager the vague total, all-told:
Shun me come time to pay up,
And shunt upon truth.

WHO, LUMUMBA?

Whose were the hands that lashed you to the tree?
Whose were the shoulders locked on barrel stock that night?
Whose knuckles beating out torture tattoo?
Whose were the chains that restrained you on that flight?
What ruffian pack of hyenas on that plane—
Copper-bound hounds, Lubumbashi Macoutes?
Who ran Katanga? Fuck Tshombe! Who ran Katanga?
Who propped up the macaque to silverback
When they needed a good imperial recruit?
I see you Washington, Langley, and Brussels,
Loot houses in Antwerp and blood banks at Bruges;
She's hot for Mandingo that Belga whore
She's got the whole map smeared with her rouge.
Who Judas-smooched you? Who wanted Congo-slow?
Who beat you with your own Chief of Staff,
Like Zulfikar hanged by his own mellow Zia?
Who hacked your baby government in half?
Who framed you again as a black-faced Marxist?
Indeed who framed you first time as a thief?
Who distorted your pan-African motivations
When you had to turn to Moscow for relief?
Even Che Guevara knew you had no time
For right wrestling left, for red grappling green,
But cold war poles piercing only extremes
Inked intrigue on everyone in between.

So who didn't see the Simba coming?
Who claimed Laurent Kabila dead?
Who skulked back to whitewash you in acid
After stealing bone bits from your head?
Who cut you up like so much stockfish?

Who tried to file your halo down?
Who the fuck handed Mobutu
That leopard insult of a crown?
When Hammarskjöld's star lit the night
Did the same nerves fire fuselage of the plane?
But never mind the bloody hands—
What frankenstein's was the bloody brain?
Who eyed central Africa chessboard style,
Playing pawns into trap-door squares?
Who didn't find modest development
To the taste of globalized affairs?
Who jumped the knights till Sunny Rawlings
Made a stew of Nkrumah's mess?
Who pressed Nigeria's rooks for union,
Spitting phlegm on Biafra's distress?

First hero of the Congolese!
First martyred by the meddlers, I call your name!
Lumumba! Who wants us to forget, to pack it in?
Who can't find a coffin box to stash their blame?
Who trussed you up and ground you into putsch?
Whose were the bonfires that seared down to tribe
Whatever dreams you had for unified Africa?
Who wouldn't let the chips fall, played the house bribe?
Whose were the hands that broke your bones in series?
Whose were the ropes that trussed you to the tree?
Whose were all the trigger finger twitches?
Who unwittingly set your legacy free?

3/   OKIGBO

A SIXTEEN FOR CHRISTOPHER OKIGBO

To the tune of Pete Rock & C.L. Smooth - They Reminisce Over You
(T.R.O.Y.) [With a nod to Tom Scott]

Poet of unimaginable talent and potential who excelled at everything,
from letters to sport. He immediately enlisted in the Biafran army,
and died in the war.

Only five when his mother died, looking in the skies
He saw the trees rising high, but he couldn't find a guide.
Sent to the genius school in Umuahia,
But he still knew how to party down underneath the raffia
They were building up the nation at the college in Ibadan.
If the classics were a bottle, he found love at the bottom.
Chopping up the lingo live with John Pepper Clark—
The Great Lion librarian on a sort of a lark.
Striving up through the trees with his charismatic verse
But he felt the country's fall to the colonial curse.
Sneezing dust from the rubble of Nzeogwu's coup
So when the war struck, he stuck out his chest, said "Guess who!"
Two weeks between the day the poet lost his duel
And the Asaba massacre where he had gone to school.
Now high above the canopy, a thunder cloud, relevant,
While craven hunters wonder at what happened to the elephant.

ÉKÉ

[To the Sacred Python]

Weave your way stillfully n'úzò
Along our footworn paths, and as often,
Along swift spirit conveyances;
Refuse the pause for gong, drum or thunder;
Probe your hands-off herald ways, harmless while
Safe on Àlà, salt-sweet mother red-breast,
Potent in revenge. Stay your wroth scale-sleight,
Your scales whose wise angles wrestle sunlight
To throw beams into bush, bent from rain cloud;
Your slither catches and magnifies slivers
From engine-grind of thought. For you Ágbàrà's
Dance would deign to halt and change direction.

Nativity sets and passion plays now undermine
Our sacred days, our crossroads in full feast;
The crucifix has usurped Ìkéngà;
Men see fit to burn your bush; lunatics
Cut your throat and call themselves martyrs.
Earth, your broad òbí lies desecrated
With splinters shivered from elders' stools.

What of this Chúkwú counterfeit in ńzú,
Who dares not eat your flesh but bids us do so?
What of my impoverished education
In your beadle tongue? How can I better learn
To recognize your urgent admonition?

There is defense to be had in self-scorn,
Invoked sparsely, at the apt time only,

But I, not even equipped with that much
Armor, am left the most constantly
Scant of ease, straining for alertness to
Ụ̀bụ̀bọ̀-m̀mụ́ọ́ poised right above my head.

Yet come time I'll take that hair gift from you,
Forfeiting liberty or life. I'll die,
Commending myself to your remembrance,
That moment my dreams first became your hostel.

Nwa Ímò m̀mírí, nwa Dím Ònyékà íyí,
You've come north to study and you're still home
Here within reach of Agwazi, Onishe,
Come into the sphere of ancient Nri, still home.
Half-skewed from Ekpo Calabar,
Ekpe Aro, Mbari Owèrrè,
You're still home but are you entirely true?

I've perhaps had to travel much farther
To come true, completely shedding home skin
To learn I still wore its very same patterns,
As long as I've kept your snake heart sheltered,
As long as I've allowed you in my dreaming
To hang your unflexed coils around my neck,
Gliding against pallid chill of sleeper sweat.
Remember how far I've come to forward
Your tidings. Know me by how earnestly
I've passed them to whomever cares to listen.

FACEFUL OF RAIN

I crave the frantic fret
Of raindrops on my cheek,
Of bead-bounce off brows,
Salt free tear-channel leak,
Of wet warp through eyelash.
Come inscrutable freight
Of sudden thunderhead,
Undo my dried-out state,
Greet me in leaf-patter,
Clacking "AQUA! AQUA!"
To thrummed earth tones,
The complicit fracas
Of soil-savvy crawlers.
Curse this sky-sport shake,
This bluesy-tint shower,
This black-bile bellyache,
Praise song soured to ballad,
To quiet storm R&B.
No more this old maudlin
Grim drift, this Simon Legree
Trip-trap at Uncle Tom's
Cabin roof from Massa sky,
This low-down cold oppressor,
Sallow-sop vault on high.
Off, armor overcoat!
Time to pen-etch ideal
Sphere music against this ditty
For pity, this song sung surreal.

I'm off south to winter,
For tropical riot rinse,

For rain the full displacement
Of air, clear evidence
That it can wait, heaven, tempest
Time kept, tattoo on tin roof,
Tripping the courtyard bucket,
Drip-testing futile reproof
Of weather-sealed cement blocks
And rattle-clack louvres,
Dry assurance of which
Architectural maneouvres
Lists losses as spider-style
Moisture-mesh prints the wall,
Calypso craquelure, Rembrandt
Of tap-tap trickster protocol,
Treating next with the slate floor,
Dot-dash on pot and calabash
Till we hear the klaxonned code,
Heed the elemental rash
And tumble out of doors,
Chasing after rana,
Opening trumpet mouths
To honeydew manna,
Splashing up dramatics—
THALÁTTA! THALÁTTA!
Jesus boys spraying pray,
Their drip-pricked stigmata.

I look for rain-ball friends
Under that mile-wide spigot.
We chip it over puddles
We heel cheeky flick-up
After inside foot swerve
Then ball follow rainbow,
Failing most times, a laugh,
Before having a go,

Lash into splash for goal,
Tonking old rhino skin
Of sodden ponder-ball
Against hydrostatic cling,
With trickle, dribble, slick touch
Drunk-skittering off ankle,
Scudding just ahead of
The long-skid slide tackle.
Nearby small-pikin squads
Play Catcher, running ripe
Mango bomb plots, kicking
Ant trails to frenzied hype,
Which lead to scatter from
The nail-dagger sharp-shot fling...
Ah WEY! four-square "Ball-U"
In the quadrangle clearing,
And here come sister-girls
Lured away from Ten-Ten
By commotion, and I too,
'Cross ocean, recalling when.

Where is that toe tap west
Here where no sunshine breaks,
Where fog patterns commerce,
Where smog hazes up stakes
Where showers are cat scrub,
Lave under yowled protest,
Health-slop slurped in a strop—
Mother Pacific knows best!
Or Plymouth Rock side east
Where diasporic jazz
Trickles from niggard cloud
To few gratified Ahs.
Where word is: *what good hope?*
To those who stole this cape,

From weatherman-shy sky
That soaks their ticker tape.
Even my home away,
This bright country on high,
Not quite Iríjí wet
Not quite Ụ́gụ̀rụ̀ dry
Gives too little action—
The summer eve monsoon
Is only a rumor
Of my true birthright June.
Speak to me, spirit twin,
In rain's teleport tongue,
Give my head the wet business
From where my green shoot was sprung.

JUNGLE BUFFALO

It's like that, ụ̀nà!

Feeling these wack rhythms of my joints cracking
Takes me back to my first pass at the steez.
Let's see you break your wrist said the loiter kids
You got that one move down, that rubber knees
MJ Wiggles move with liquid L at elbow.
Now show us you can lock it out proper;
Hit that wave on freeze and let it go.

Nothing like training the snap at tension to get
Your joints producing your own supply of juice,
Long before conjecture of opiate receptors
The fresh kids knew they could boogaloo for the boost.
You gotta get down to gorilla up like shorty King Kong.
Show me love by the crony call: yes yes y'all!
       It took the beat and the breaks to teach me how to belong.

Know how much practice I totted up popping?
Had my maths teacher saying: *Uche, you scatter*
Your body one more time in my class, I'll have you cutting grass
For twelve hours. But how you get superpowers doesn't matter
As long as when a punk kid shows you up to prove,
You can light him up like a Shell pipeline gas flare.
Better get your fly cape on when needle sweeps the groove.

Loiter kids said *ńgwá! that's ice but what up*
With the throwdown? Where's that go-hard on cardboard?
Shoot, I even had uprock all in my toprock
And these cats wanted more than whiplash spinal cord?
You know, like Beat Street, they said, and spun Frantic Situation.
After all that, undone by the Zulu Nation ululation.

Alright, bet I'm back with the low, low down gyration.
    It took the beat and the breaks to teach me how to belong.

Once you've hit up pineal gland for kite chemicals
It's time to whisk the inner ear for special blends.
Start with the backspin on the semicircular
Curricular, then crank up the scramble till the ankle sends
It kneespin, handspin, helicopter, crabwalk,
And—do you dare—headspin. There was rumor of a kid
Who had the windmill down, but that was no battle, tall talk.

Saturday night, the norm kid set step-skanking
To standard boogie, Shalamar, Kool and the Gang,
We pressed reject, dodging prefects, helped our boy
Over the fence with bootlegged ghetto-blaster to hang
Out under boom-bap in the empty classrooms all night long.
Good thing we had no Krylons or we'd be long odds for not
    expelled.
    It took the beat and the breaks to teach me how to belong.

Not for me money for Kangol and shell-toes,
A striped track suit for mufti would be contraband.
The laugh question is how fly I could pimp the design
Of an unironed school uniform. Once I could land
A kip-up after cold pose to close the floor routine,
Wrap up pop-lock, stock and barrel, brush down apparel;
Even wearing dirty, stand hard that moment clean.

Everything a B-Boy knows for pain strikes back
In lightning of the five elements. It's no joke the opium
A kid needs to get through the drama of bullies,
Nut-cracker prefects, teachers always scoping him
And girls not. There's no muscle like buffalo stance strong.
An age past those moves, I still peep fam the damn world over.
    Word. Took the beat and the breaks to teach me how to belong.

LE FREAK MUSIQUE AFRIQUE

He's not at home, nor should he be,
Okéké in the ballroom, over sea.

Yé-kpa! Sound check in the pocket,
Rimshot fanfare—stick up to rock it,
That's the whole band, one foot left
To half-step then down the right to bless,
Hips the vibe's half-loop wide
Over sharp, square shoes in stride,
Where smooth soles get the slither,
Under masquerade gun to deliver
For goddess of red earth and naked feet.
Say we all say once on the beat,
Then the shift is on, syncopo-stitch-up,
Instinctive sway against the stave's stirrup,
From temperate canter through Tropic of Cancer
So into the groove of Sahel latitude.
Stay with them, audience, follow audacity
On bobbing waves in rude-buoyed odyssey,
Walk off the chronic at the front of frolic,
At the brocaded border of baroque.
Stay with them, audience, by the left, kick march
Èkpè, nri! Èkpè, ńrí! Èkpè, ńrí!
Commot for road oh! Commot for road!
Èkpè, ńrí! Èkpè, ńrí! Company...halt!

Not sure how far, or should he reach at all,
Okéké, for the folk tale's prodigal.

Love Nwantinti! Solo by pick-head
Bowed over palm wine guitar, sozzled

In brew of the thing-string plucked lightly,
Soffri-soffri, that's for where they sing.
Tori knacked down from savannah town,
Told loosely, like warp strand of horn ranks,
Like the digit stressing borrowed guitar fret,
Told by lip pressed twitter across river banks,
By ọ̀jà, twin-tone flute of song after sweat,
Told for tapper atop, tethered in, alert
To the current through canopy, ion bird
Past electron leaf and corn row circuit,
Told in sweat bled from cut glass of capsicum,
Mixed in with ụgụ́ and waterleaf upon yam.
Gbam! So back from dreamland the beat lands,
Rocking punts on the purled flow through mangrove,
Past scalloped shores, each note enslaved, a shrove
Plea, a beckoning to the giant rock
By the causeway, a palm-out socket
For dharma milked from desert djinn demesne
By drummer, by dibị̀à dika Dibango,
To beat of strobe flashes (I bless the rains),
Hands up to conduct, fingers to finagle,
Thighs to thicken, belly out to swag,
Toes in their throe down while, en masse, en vague,
Up the arms, and down drummer—get some!—
Tambours taking on the fast-talk of rag,
Ears tweaked near to tintinnabulation.
More fire, more fire, quakes the amplifier
Ògéné gong to blast off from Babylon.

Behind his shut eyes: bush, and then he's lost,
Okéké, in the Black Night pentecost.

Encore! It's tumbas against the floorboard,
Battery of massed footfalls chord after chord,
Opening call for ùdù's throat-sung response;

Then further on, didgeridoo bonny
Over the ocean, all along where even
The sea floor raves under tsunami.
Come djembe, come bottom funk, beating
Down brows in mother-of-salt secretions,
Come mortar and pestle, the pre-meal thump,
Come throw-down and wrestle, crescendoing crunk.
Clap-bang tattoo against bushmeat skin,
Come over she-choir, tombside ululation,
Come over playing ten-ten, clap for pikin,
Tim-bom-tim-bom, boys kalaba, titi alaba boom!
Come over bayou, two-step Tchoupitoulas.
Can they hang, all puntu and citrus tang,
Before the juju clergy, candle lit,
Leaping hot blush over the crowd's flush.
It's written: the polite parker interdict,
So come fat-belleh bailiff, big monkey man,
Eye out not for contraband spliff in hand,
But for sacrilege of rooted buttock.
Only skitter of electron feet conduct
That canopy, jake's laddering of charge
Down gallery bald heads on circuit march
Èkpè, nri! Èkpè, ńrí! Èkpè, ńrí!
Up the crazy têtes brulées on stage,
Come on the freak frequency, come on blaze
Of ìrókò mask eyes (ọ́jị̀ m̀ḿanwú ọ́jọ́ọ́),
Of íkòrò tempo (carry ya ǹjàkị̀rị̀),
Come on ichor of the gods we truly live for,
Bring us from our mother muse with one more
Jungle motet before the mowers make naked the floor.

Move us inside music to script our memento.
Move us into the mood, for music is the moon
In movement meeting the mute nuisance of midnight evil.

Some bible blighters mutilated
Some murmuring from muezzins mutilated
Some bullet machines mutilated
Our mutual song and sung-back.
But we are the multitude, and our memento is music and
    movement.
Our mutiny is the moon in movement.
Dance with us—egwu! Or drag along in your darkness.
Our rhythms are the richness. Our footfalls full ground.

Communion calls, so ever far away and flung;
Okéké, full of grace, receives his mother tongue.

TWO-VOICED FLUTE

Play on, flute of the twin voices,
Oh shy, two-tone harmonizer,
Throaty foundation,
Oh floor to extend under any
    Wandering trajectory
      Of the song's feet.

Garrulous double,
    Taiwo of tall echo
With a full hand's collection
      Of tones,
Translator for the sacred bush of ghosts.
Even in this land where the
    Plants have been
      Pressed into metamorphic
      Grains of sand.

Taken together, a compass
    With the artist's emblem at the angle
A mason with a perfect
    Standing
Corner
    At
The heels.

But a less logical angle
    At the hand hold below
      The ambiguous mouthpiece:
        Raw earth stirred with water requires room
          For width of a mammal's pulse.

Adobe.
Jìdéòbí.
Adobe.
Jìdéòbí.

Two branches carrying in their xylem
    The flow from twin tributaries,
        Ímò ḿmírí and Colorado.

The spaceship lights have dot-dashed the message from frogland,
Throaty foundation
    Of water.
        The Bonny Bight over the ocean.
        The Bonny Bight over the sea.
        Oh bring back Biafara to me.
And from doldrum Atlantis the dual in the message:
        Two-tone flute, garrulous, speaking
            For untold, mute ghosts.

They gather to gawk at this
Roomful of travelers
        Before plucking
        My ear's nerve
            With recognition,
        Then
            Right as I turn
                The Doppler shapes dipper,

Attenuating
Into their lovely pairs.

MYSTIC DRUMMALOGUE

A Colloquy. Italicized are excerpts from "The Mystic Drum"
by Gabriel Okara

The mystic drum beat in my inside
fishes danced in the rivers...

I am massive! Beating on Earth with drum licks
True to trunk my elephant calls to hippo,
Struts vibrating beds of the fish demesnes, Boom!
Feel my baton! Bap!

standing behind a tree...

Thunder braces roots wheresoever trees tap
Groundling passions; forests are drawn blinds
Over mysteries even the drum cannot pierce—
Blindfolded magic.

...leaves around her waist...

Thighs in bark, deciding my range with bow shot,
Breasts like morning offering to Mother Earth, milk,
Nectar, palm wine, water and pepper all mixed,
Dashed in my pupils.

...she only smiled with a shake of her head...

Stricken! Shot by innocence, furled to missile
Strength, the drummer desperately measures beat-box
Fury—Gbuum! Bamboozled, my quarry? No? Here's Gbam!
How do you hold out?

...trees began to dance
the fishes turned men
and men turned fishes...

Brother wood of medicine, hear me! Shake out
What you harbor! Press her my way! I know your
Ransom. I'll drum blur into bounds of gods, lands,
Waters and species.

...then the mystic drum
in my inside stopped...

What have I done? What this alarum? Whose strides
Echo ancient purpose my way? I daren't
Learn the true costs tallied in blows at finger
Fillips of chaos!

...roots sprouting from her
feet and leaves growing on her head

Nothing done now can disentangle this thatch,
Bring the soft fruit back from her hardened wood stock;
Even drumbeat won't introduce my mage-might
Seed to her body.

Then, then I packed my mystic drum
and turned away; never more to beat so loud.

Killed me softly; she has me limp in new earth,
Quiet and soon in slumber I nod to a slowed beat.
What the hunter chases sometimes consumes him,
Becomes him forever.

He comes and becomes
He comes and becomes
He comes and becomes
He enters the womb
He has entered, wounded
The womb becomes him forever

FORTUNE OF CHÍ

When those two fighters met at the horizon
Half pregnant with yellow sun as it rose
And fell at once to Schrödinger degree,
They spun so much imperfection of soul
And circumstance into their tumbled dice
That its sum could be none other than me,
Quantum twin unleashed from edge of the black hole—
I am perfected fortune of my Chí.

Some randomized permutation of genes
Spelled these very left and right brain cortices—
Green-lit my nerves with sheer possibility;
Some Mendel melody conjured these eyes,
These muscles, grafted these veins under this skin;
I am too many pin-point faults to be
By design yet I crown my own life's fitness:
I am perfected fortune of my Chí.

But that same line some call a thread of fates
To which I fit my mind and body's curve
In its degrees is certainly not free;
Somewhere along its future lies a point
Where my arrival is the landing of lots,
Thrown onward into rightful symmetry;
I am the series that evolves to that clinch:
I am perfected fortune of my Chí.

ROAD TO ONITSHA, 1989

The journey is a litany bold-writ
In parchment, dry and sunburnt at the edges,
Inscribed with a newly ragged people's
Million offered prayers and ritual signs,
A people who've seen enterprise through shuttered
Eyes but when unblinkered found shadow where
Onitsha's coal and lumber had once torch-lit
The Niger's banks, now choked with compounds
Whose owners squat grub-shacked, back to back, itched
Alert, sending pseudopods far north and west;
A shade world, equatorial opposite
Of Las Vegas, raised from nothing desert.
Here the spread-hamlet governed jungle
Entails an ornate mirage of bounty,
Fleecing just as surely those who are drawn
To its seemingly market-tested mystique.

Such charming euphony where bristling palms
Bustle-up wind tones under puddled skies,
Such caesure in the jarring from potholes!
Termitariums warting the road-flank soil
Seem as if tunneled to the antipode,
Such their stature and apparent age;
They certainly inspire my suspicions
That their denizens in their fated time
Will undermine and thus inherit the earth.
Or has that time indeed already come?
Approaching a wasteful phalanx of stealthy
Limousines and coughing luxury buses,
Who is to say this iroko citadel,

Gateway to the grandmotherlode forest
Is still under control of the two-legged?

Through the window I feel the lacerations
Slashed through hills to lay commercial track.
What red-blooded creature could stand
To make such gashes in a mother's flesh,
Exposing gore in heaps prone to slide across
The winding tar? What individually
Sensible being would leave off clean razor
For match, would immolate green bed of his own
Sustenance come time for cultivation?

Further in the background the canopy
Shows signs of malnourishment from heavy
Monoculture, Nitrogen flight leaving
The soil nothing but its acid, which rains
A vengeance on zinc roofing (i̩ màgo,
Acid takes its shortest shift with metal).
What son of man's miracle redeems
The loss of topsoil from those fret-work hills?
Shrives the bare trees that shriek their ghost loneliness?
Purges the defecation from construction,
Sand in mounds, gravel in heaps, cement blocks
Set up as if mass-manufactured tombs,
Ordure on a deserted stretch, perverted
Signs of the local food chain, but without
The vulture's iconic baldhead, no-fool's cap
On full stop. Local enterprise cuts sharp grains
From the riverbanks, and the poison wind
Is trade driven on without the first thought
Of commonwealth, of sustainability.

There's littlest margin for compromise
At the boundary, parley point between
Arcadian marketplace and shantytown.
From rainforest lore which made some use
Of every material, every effect,
Even shrouded fears, even death, the way
Is now built to stand well off consequence.
This road swerves to avoid what yam barn stocks
Still rely on bunched-iron calves and forearms,
On craftily bluffed smoke of rainmakers,
Not least on raveling threads of mystery
From the great masquerades, on all these ancient
Engine blocks of festival season, steeped
In Igbotic oil of purest Capital.
Such old settings cow the carriageway's sponsors,
The socios, yellow kerosene lamp flames
Who layer obfuscating soot on the stained
Collage glass of Temple One Nigeria.
Best to shun age-old enterprise, dismantle
The market in its purest form, print cash
While ignoring the stubborn samizdat
Of ongoing smallholder traditions.
After all, at this greyscale rainbow's end
A cathedral bourse of legend will rise
To service the New World Bund (All hail!)
Or is all that construction of a bubble
Film-skinned with global arbitrage, measured
In terms of banknotes stuffed under mattresses
Within gated, glass-shard-topped compound walls?

Nostalgia is never more a sweetened dose
Of nepenthe than when wheels ease you past
The landmarks of your return home long ago.
You blink away the clues in every scene
That you've no real future, scion of intellectual

Parvenus here where meritocracy's
Most earnest champions have met the chill steel
Interruption of well-oiled guillotine.
Suddenly I'm faced with a backmasking
Of Donaldson's "Land of my Birth", the song
That ushered me homeward over the bridge
Ten well-stocked years ago. It's a message
I hear while sitting poised upon the bitts,
A message at the journey home's bitter end,
A message encoded into the rush
Of agberos through fetid motorparks,
In the rubbish heaped upon roundabouts
(Such sacrilege in a land that understands
The utter sanctity of a crossroads!)
Those are ugly things behind our car
There is a mess on either side of us
There comes ahead the cesspool of Lagos,
Beyond that the émigré's uncertainty
Or limbo should the bid for visa fail.
I'm resigned in my well-trained wise of exit.
Truth has failed its potential and lies in
This gross chimaera of a patch-scrap state.

Unless the windscreen is a warped mirror
Slandering the federal character of beauty.

ROAD FROM CALABAR TO ABUJA

Shot out through the newly-set stelae
Welcoming to Calabar, we plunge into
Lucent green: chlorophyll to brimming,
Pale blue vessel clapped over our heads,
Illumined to reflect forth in the chipped, black strip of road;
Jagged mounds astride the shoulder teem with ants.

Into the gentle basins of the delta bread basket—
Sour sop lollipop land. Akamkpa now Ikom and
Combs of coconut with wavy leaves of plantain,
Fan leaves of cocoyam, and hardwoods strutting the sky.
Mounds astride the shoulder are muscular yam
Winding into razor plots of pineapple.

Past Ogoja into Benue, grass reaching to pull down
Tree tops—brown streaked green
Of banana stands under these bowed crowns
Mounds astride the shoulder are cassava spreads.
Round cement huts topped with thatch
Bon-boy bobbing heads mark paneless windows.

Gboko to Makurdi, trees step lightly over
Rioting grass. Dust motes laze gnat-like in still air.
Mounds astride the shoulder are stock of citrus vendors,
Suspiciously, for December, occasional usurp of mangoes.
Orange orchards march out from the red canvas
Against whites and purples of thick sugarcane.

Copper, rust, straw of new construction—
Mounds astride the shoulder are sterile brick heaps,
Savannah grain stacks drying, cleared bush

Over the Benue, grey waters bitten by
Brown sand bars (Cameroon courtesy in silt),
White cows kicking up brown clods and dust spray.

Mounds astride the shoulder are fresh quarried granite,
Laborers stooping over stone slabs in the sun
Black columns of burning bush spring from the horizon
Ash waste flats on denatured brown
Rearing up past Akwanga, heaving hills, slashing dips,
And uncertain, green clumps that cling on dear.

Year-round harmattan palette—
Trees full wizened to brush—
The mounds are Capital Rock...

RAINBOW CITY PRESAGE OF STORM

heaven's drooping face was drest
In gloomy thunderstocks: earth, seas, arrai'd
In all presage of storm...

—George Chapman

Somehow even interned here, outer urban
Space, long before I sense the skies have been
Dimming ever incrementally, comes
A queer sense, retro-firm now in fine-comb
Memory, that I walk in rain forest,
Unmarred by metro filth or hulking rust.
The illusion waxes when I approach
A street corner and withers otherwise,
As if a transparency is breathing
Enchanted air through our blighted atmosphere.
The unreal uncity is wilderness
With clay paths through giant green, wet flowing crease,
And teat duct of roots into nursery soil.

I stop, stunned still by the electricity
Of these superimposed signals through my nerves.
Newly sensitive, I catch a sudden beam
Of ghost fire from a quickly sickening sun
Through its hospital bedsheet of leaden cloud;
The world's sap is sunk, I see, and thunderheads
Cast down anemic limbs, discolored beams
To herald their growth into the wetwork.
They grunt in elemental labor; here comes
Rain to gulp the world in native fury;
Midwife winds descend with a wild swing.
Whoopsa! they cry quite out sympathetic.

We've been repositioned by missionaries
To rage against each droplet's imp; to brood
In cultivated melancholia, mimic
Jonathan Swift's wit to cavil against
The entrails of our towns when water bloat
Exposes them; to take no less than the rains
As some marauding foe lain siege on our walls
Of proud invention, to waive our birthright
Old arts, arch tropic powers from long study.
We're losing the rainmaker prerogative;
We come to prefer mansion masonry,
To make for ourselves mere pokes of stuffed air.

The troposphere is no common cavalry;
Its triumphs are triple rainbows afterward,
But first it charges with a mania far
Beyond our force and intuition: Its whirled
Reserves find every chink in our clapped world.
We've taken up a march of regiments
Called by a foreign general. *Stand fast*
Against flies that pepper your pelts in bloodhunt.
Stand fast against their spawn in market gutters
Wriggling raindrop disco. Stand fast against
The unseen squatter imps who bore potholes
Into roadway macadam, against muck
That dances green phalanges up your walls,
Plaque algae on poxed paint, smut clusters
On red earth paths where black loam lost hold,
Red rust on antique iron contrivances.
Stand fast against root-rot of land denuded
By bush fires and nonrotated farms
Until bluffs of deradicalized soil
Slide meekly away, silting the rivers.
Stand fast against disease which works fierce progress
From overflowing Sulo bins of waste,

Through carcasses of bloated animals,
And not always animals, washed through streets
By flash floods — exhibit A: the stock fate
Of rebels. Stand fast! Shake off the shell-shock
Take quinine pill chaw and snootfuls of snuff.
Stand fast, you chew-stick white teeth in red gums
On black hide. Where be green besides mucus?
Send your left/right against the pest heavens;
Bed in, I said! Cement! Metal! Stand fast!

We good soldiers have first learned to forget
Our genotype armor, waterproof skin.

The wind that topples over power poles,
That puts the shiver into loose louvres,
Drives me homeward in procession from town
To outskirt bush and checker-plot hamlets,
Into lush country of weed among
The waterleaf, maize and cassava,
Plantain shoots closing rank into mews
Of wooded risers, sprawling, tender stalks,
Periscoping infant leaves through dense mulch,
Mould of greying towers, scarred ìchékú,
Black-gummed holes on white boles of iroko.
Outside my house swamp-spawned elephant grass
Chokes its dainty cousin, creeping fern grows
Into dendrite cracks below my window.
The titter of nameless coastal birds braid tune
With rough bass toad—from whom rainmen attain
Their craft. Above all, the clouds in dark freight
Paint the nude metals below in damp fright,
Shoot lightning to fête the tropic rapture,
And groan their swollen cells until these rupture,
Ụ́dárà plump-peeled, their sweet wetness pinch-drained...
Then suddenly heaven itself slants down.

ÌGBÒ DIRECTIONS IN AMSTERDAM

Eh! Excuse me young man; you look Nigerian.

I am, I say, I am indeed.

OK good. I thought you were going to speak Dutch to me
How can people understand that yè yé language?
Kai! They just cut their throat all the time:
Gracht! Gracht! Gracht! Tùfiá-kwà!
So therefore, where are you from, now?

I'm from America, visiting from Colorado.

Nonsense! Which kind answer be that?
Where are you **from**?

I'm from Umunakanu, Ehime, Mbano.

Eh heh! Did I not know?
Kèdú ka í mèrè?

Ọ́ dị ḿmá!

Eh heh! So you speak your language.
I na suo Ìgbò.
I wasn't sure with that supri-supri accent.
Me, I'm from Nnewi.

And so she switched to rapid, riverside Ìgbò,
Drawing me along on the Niger at the Onitsha bridge,
Almost sweeping me across to Anioma.

I held on, half drowned and gasping;
Finally, a snatch of shore.

Á nàm a chọọ Regulierswahrsstrasse.
Ọ nwèrè ónyé na e nyèlúm áká ébáà-hu.
Bíkò, i nwéére íhé díkà map?

I held out my second-hand Amsterdam op de Fiets
With its regimented blocks of pleins upon grachts.
Smiling as she squinted at the slip of paper from her purse
The misspelled Dutch.
Who had tried to drown her
This far from Onishe's care?
Who had commended her,
So far from her paradise of jí,
To the alien currents of the Ij?

DEAR BONNY, DEAR BIAFARA,

My many trips through your waters where waves
And tides pinch-mold the Niger and its Cross
Nephew taught me the tongues my father's rich
Loam supplied, as did my mother's spice board.

My schooling to your near north pointed across
The Sahel, the Sahara, the Med, where rich
Migration called, the graduate "All Aboard!
Globalization Express!" Amber waves

Of grain here near north of Pike's Peak, enriched
Despite greater practice with snowboard
Than fishing canoe on my homeland waves,
The River Niger and the River Cross.

Your grace waives my having crossed your generous
Board, far from your dole yet somehow still enriched.

PRAYER BEFORE WRITING

Bless me chí na álúsí, in one way, at least:
Guide the hand that gathers timber to build
For all neighbors, lovers and comers houses.
There's so much labor in learning the joints
In learning the swings that turn shape into wood
So much watching for what form arouses
The prime instincts of living from my clients.

Save me from the blazes of my own causes.

I speak to others of carpenter market
Some have chopped away the shadows from trees
They've chopped a lacquer of sap unto their trousers
They've chopped through splinters, ébí ógwù bath
Chopped the tongues from bearers of news
Chopped the wet fingers from lovers and spouses
Chopped off the staff-holding hands of old priests.

Save me from the blazes of my own causes.

Bless me chí na álúsí, if in this sole way:
Brace me with trust in my fastens and joints
As they were true joints as the true joint dowses
Don't let me chop that it's only the chopping
Let me put people in homes from whole legend
Spare them the breakdown to stops and clauses.
Until I'm lain prone on my own cut lintel,
Save me from the blazes of my own causes.

A SIXTEEN FOR THE DIASPORA

*To the tune of Nas — The World Is Yours [DJ Premier, with love
to Ahmad Jamal]*

For the seed on trade wind, children of Àlà and her sisters. We full ground!

My mind rises, no double-Cross, on the Niger, river with the
    hard R
Vibing, we Naija people work to the top while rocking hard scars
Beats bobbing in our hearts tell the stalwarts where the bars are,
Our cousins who've kept it popping long since their kidnap off the
    sandbars
Plotting for freedom on the seas a million leagues from Zanzibar
Taking all the degrees; who thought we'd take consciousness this
    far
When they melted our history down, looted our worth to the tune
    of Europe first
Now we're after the Earth and after that the universe
Ridden world circles on wooden then steel ships, airplane
    wingtips
Coming back round for your culture, your grand larcenized
    benefits
Putting our minds up in your science; scribing jive to rewrite your
    language,
Not only the slang but even the twang rhythm your kids' tongues
    bang with.
We dedicate the mindstate of settlement to rivers on the home
    Continent
Seal memories in reveries with funk sent up from the fundament.
When we sing we mean every song as a strong swim to oblige her
Leave the safekeeping of what we forget to sweet brown silt of the
    Niger.

4/ ŃCHÉFÙ ROAD

ŃCHÉFÙ ROAD

for Victor Okigbo

I

In the bustling days of Chou
The Old Philosopher set out.
Stopped many times, each time he knew
Afresh the weariness and doubt
That forced him from renowned Luo-Yang,
Whose influence thrust out from Zhou
Through later dynasty of Tang.
He fumed: *They're quite the same, aren't they?*
While hurrying past admiring gaze,
The greed for wealth and for knowledge,
The savant's vice is ever praise.
He pressed forth to the border post;
Warden requested a book for the wise,
Though Laozi favored his fleeting host,
His words emerged shīfu surprise:

> *Yin Hsi, my friend, eagerness for wisdom*
> *Lies heavily upon your rugged shoulders —*
> *You the most attuned to recognize truths.*
> *Look you outward from this frontier posting;*
> *To wilderness sprawling beyond the walls.*
> *Though you batter them with profound proverbs,*
> *Birds and fish feed wildly in their whereabouts;*
> *Come tigers and wolf packs in famished times*
> *Do you beat them away with wit or clubs?*
> *Would the gnomic kennings of nature's riddles,*
> *Of dawn and dusk, of ebb and tide,*
> *Of drought and flood set these in your power?*

Look not towards court intellects
Lest you join in their dry vanity:
Look outward with a humble gaze.
Look to me: ageing man, uncertain journey.
> *Wisdom is harsh, and men don't apprehend it.*

In the library at Nsukka I found
Not only the Ìgbò and Efik Bibles
But more of my childhood cosmology
Which meant I'd never be a disciple.

Quark and Gilgamesh, Popul Vuh and mc^2
My brain, bent by anthropics and Upanishads
Found in the Dàodé Jīng a wheel to affix
So many worldly poles at fearsome odds.

Nile, Niger, Senegal, Congo, Orange, Limpopo, Zambezi.
Congo or Chambeshi, Ubangi-Uele plus Kasai—
There is no territory, so never mind the map.

II
Ńchéfù Road is untarred.
The dust my sandals raise
Drifts slackly back down
to settle in my footprints,
Joining my growing grist
Of spent skin cells
Washed by muddled humors,
Moving waters within
And immediately without me.

Some time after the first canal, I awoke.
I wandered the waters; I wandered the roads.
Ńchéfù Road has no courtesy signs
I might be at Nsukka; I might be at Calabar

There is no structure of memory,
Of hard pitch under my foot soles.
Ńchéfù Road is untarred.

That unstable wake,
That left behind evanescence,
Traces upon traces, is somehow also
My ambition, a unicellular
Layer of words that were
And words destined to be.

It's blasphemy to tread here
Weighted down with
The old skin's whispers.
The first nonsense
I failed to unload
At the headwaters
Is the youthful solipsism
That I tread here alone.

Ńchéfù Road is a parallel
Universe of penitents—
The way behind me scarred,
Footprints covered up again,
Body pits covered up again;
I wouldn't know those few
Who persevered from those numerous
Who drowned in traps the size
Of whatever mirrors they carried
With them in their pockets.
I expect at any moment to succumb,
Stuck in my own head's height
Of babbling slough
Under false grey topping
Of unicellular thickness.

(In the beginning prokaryotes,
In the end prokaryotes again.)

The road has nor beginning nor end,
Ouroboros of Ocean, Ímò and Íyí.
Many gallants have died
Plotting the course along which
Migrant spirits glide its length.

But Ńchéfù Road is not for answers;
It guides you only through the wisdom
You repeat to yourself in mirrors
Carried along in your pockets,
Only through your personal tributary.
It babbles to drown out noise
Of your walking wake with
a hundred handed-down tales
Tucked into hard corners
Of sharply conflicting morals,
Each of which it enforces
At some time, in some way,
In some lawless, sudden chaos.

The road is thoroughfare
Of legion community daimons;
You lose yourself in cogitation,
You bend to take your measurements,
To press the leaf in your book,
To press the insect in your book,
To press the carcass of an overheard
Proverb or song in your book,
Only to risk being overtaken
By Ékpè and Ágbàrà;
You pause to praise Ányánwụ
Only to be tripped at toe level

By the sly tendrils of her bushmates,
Only to be buried with your wise unwise.

Because along Ńchéfù road
Is—here! Sere-skin desert,
Is—here! Native hair savannah,
Is—here! Muscle-red stone,
Is—here! Scatter-limb forest,
Is—here! Digital mangrove.
Five digits—a harsh hand that slaps
Its wisdom across your cheek.
Ńchéfù Road is aorta
Of Pángǔ's equatorial twin,
The titan body continent,
Each vivid cell a daimon.

Armchair explorers weld their eyes
On their tattered, soaked and inked-up prize.

III

Whatever happened to hippopotamus?
There was a goddess of underwater thunder,
More solid than god randoms of E.G. Parrinder.
She has not capsized my boat of market goods lately—
Good for commerce, catastrophic for later commerce.

Her large-bodied lacuna is a palsy
On the planet of trade.
Without her oversight the fakery of foreign goods
Has overwhelmed Onishe
Has overwhelmed Aba.

The metalsmiths of Awka have fiddled more pig dross into their
    wares
The alien cassava has swallowed nine of ten tables in the grains
    quarter
Blackness has waned from the earth, earth gone all redbone
All because there is no hippopotamus to rise out of the Niger
And swallow up a third of the quarters spreading iniquity
All because there is no hippopotamus to rise out of Ímò.
All because there is no hippopotamus to rise out of Oyono.

With hippopotamus missing,
Shell Corp sticks a trocar in the Niger's carotid,
The brain nexus of the broad delta
Has gone desperate with dementia.

The rain forests are a poisoned harvest of dead soldiers,
The channels of shifting sand and silt
Have been spliced with hardened arteries of crumbling cement.
The loam is infected with a green muck of lurgy.
All because there is no hippopotamus
To rise out of the Afara lattice of riverine tribal skin slashes.

Whatever happened to hippopotamus?
The giants have been poisoned
By a more cowardly variety of hunters.
Where has elephant gone—ényí
Where has hippopotamus gone—ényí-ḿmírí
Already the hunters are talking about cassava
Already the hunters are talking about potatoes
Genius of the land, Genius of the water,
Help these hunters become once again adept
Help them remember thunder!

Only elephant can haul water elephant from her river
Only the poet can coax return of elephant

To coax the return of water elephant.
The muscled man, the wrestler,
Was a failure, an unmistakable failure.
He put on his barrel belly at Dodan Barracks
He murdered Mother Ransome-Kuti at Alagbon Close
He took his pot-bellied slick of petrol to Abuja;
He gloried sickly over the river warden,
Over ényí-ḿmírí, the great endangered,
By planting seeds of the river's disease.
The poet knows the wrestler's story;
Only the story sings hope of its own undoing.

IV
Mungo Park foretold his own drowning

> *I observe without hesitation*
> *That discontinuance of the slave trade*
> *Would be of beneficial effect*
> *Given the unenlightened state of mind*
> *Among Africa's native races.*

Listen, I too have judged disease
Without consideration of flesh,
With over-presumption of mind.
I'm one of those benighted natives
Supposedly more sinned against
Than sinful, supposedly noble.
What razors me from those
Who sniff at gente sin razon?
Mungo Park came across
Know-it-all ocean, a Nostromo,
Playing to the colonial gallery.
Native as I am, I wander
Down the road, unstrung for less.

Park caught his seasoning
In Pisania, his brow burned,
Tallow-torched in alien air;
He thought himself a splendid Scot
To weather the fever while heroically
Swotting the local flora,
Fauna, geography, tongues,
And customs, to foot first
The outset of his long adventure.
He also confused the fool's dundering
With stoutness of constitution.
It wasn't long before he was
Languishing in Moorish prison,
Not long thereafter desert thirst
Drove him to blows with
The ghostly boxers of mirages.
He pressed as best he could
His chalked-up maps to the unkind
Realities of granite territory.

Foolhardy sharps of the Sahel,
Wrung from their roots by cowries,
Baubles and rusted musketry
Showed Park every
Device of foul brigandage
Their myopia could conjure.
The river Niger waited, patient.

Finally at Segou, she gazed
With a billion-faceted eyes
At this self-styled prodigal,
This Calvinist impresario.
The madness not quite yet set in,
He broke off in sensible despair
He marched back

Mock darkened
Of dark countenance
To Gambian Pisania in company
Of a coffle of captives whose benighted
Native trader saw
In the European appurtenance
A mirror no larger than himself
And declared: "Black men are nothing."

The Niger, infinitely patient, bided her time.
Park returned to leisurely teas
And earnest scholar societies
But she never left his highland heart—
She gurgled through his dalliance.

The company named the coast for gold,
Old Midas, starved, half dead from cold.

V

The next time Park arrived
He put on khimairan cryptoform—
Head of imperial tri-leonine
Of voracious Georgian manticore,
Torso of stubborn highland goat,
Of billiard-ball digestion,
Tail of hundred-headed hydra,
Of blitz-delivered venom.
He chose a detachment of renegade guns
Setting out to break the thick necks
Of the petty, pilfering potentates
Of his earlier experience.

A jumper backs from a previous start
To trade momentum into spring:
Park made his landing at Goree

And hurtled past Pisania;
But nothing hurries in the tropics.
His company of jobbers, thieves, deserters,
Whose eagerness he quite mistook,
Unfurled their banner early;
The party themselves would prove
The strutting feet of his self-curse.
It should have served to warn him
That not one black man would go along.

White men defy microbial hell
With mercury and calomel.

Park came upon the river at Bamako
This time, upstream of Segou,
Nine of ten of his motley
Dead or dying of ague,
Including all his carpenters.
But he was a wretch espying afar
A desert crook shimmering false relief.
He lost his mind to febrile joy,
Announcing his bold intention
To slash out the middlemen—
From trans-Saharan caravans,
To sell guns at a cut rate.

The Niger bobbed its patience,
Neutral to this effrontery.

Having no boatwrights remaining
Park fever-fashioned
The potemkin schooner Joliba,
From wooden canoes rotting in the shallows.
In dedicating this vessel with the river's
Mandinka name, he sought her matronage.

Naiveté sang him a splendid song
While in grip of his megrim vision:
Her swifts would bear him to her trunk
Her width would thwart hostility
From fiefdoms at her varied shores
By whom bribes were civility.

Sansanding, Djenné, Tombouctou,
Left lead and arrows in the gunwhale,
Redeemed in frantic rifle shot
And quite uncalvinist curses.
Every toll he refused to pay
Compounded his boasts against the brigands.

Great Gao of past imperium
Washed past as chiseling excerpts of Touaregs
Saw a mirror the size of themselves
And declared all white men savage beasts.
Their children would get the irony.

Cut glass Sahel economy
Born bloodlust of Sonni Ali.

VI

Mungo Park swept on into Hausaland;
He crossed one double-crossing chief too far.
The troops gathered in ambush
On the banks at Bussa rapids,
Which would have been last
Before the river's great trunk,
Roots in unplumbed delta wealth
And world-winding glory of open ocean.

Park and company abandoned
The schooner and sprang into the true Joliba;

There she struck, folding bodies down
Over feet stuck between her stones.
Every man perished,
Save the guide Ahmadi,
The only one of the party
Who had no school in swimming.

Park swallowed his full
Displacement weight of river,
A mocking face in his mirror
("Black men are nothing.")
The river took him in her gullet,
A million man-sized mirrors
Distorted with lore of Bannockburn.

She saw the coming colony,
The coming arrogance of engineers,
The overcolony after that
Of Paris Club chessmasters
Who inspired fists to close
Around her throat: Kainji dam,
Despoilment at her delta
In pursuit of oil—treachery
Visited by the very natives she raised.
This was no hap. Park's final
Suffering was her comforting.

More of her comforting was the suffering
Of the townspeople at Bussa,
Visited by diseases of devilish macabre
After contact with Park.
Take care not to touch the whites
lest you perish like our people.

The Niger quest claimed Park's son
As well, doubting Thomas who died
Of fever on his own first foot,
Chasing after hope of his father's life.

Churchfolk squint at passion plays
On Harmattan's intensest days.

VII
Ńchéfù Road holds court over the Sahel
And sports through red clay and loam,
Governing life in her shallow pools,
Death in her eddies and tows.
Boring through rock and snatching at limbs
With red of iron salts and blood
Where she bends back from the Sahara.

Park was one of many after her legends;
Others probed at the Bonny Bight
Where my mother's people and my father's
Lived fluidity of interplay
Lived Dàodé Jīng flavors—
All swallowed up by Leviathan.
Leviathan who probed at first
With out-barbels for man-flesh,
For gold and ivory, stoking the fire
Of wars around Calabar, Arochukwu,
Abiriba and deep in the hinterlands,
Up from the Gulf of Guinea,
Bight of Bonny, Bight of Biafara.

Leviathan lumbered up-river—
So much more to swallow
Having tenderized the meat
With barrage from the gunboats.

That numpty Charles Marlow
Reporting from mouth of the Congo
Suffered a bankruptcy of imagination.
We lay at the other end
Of those aimless shell blasts
Into green under green of bush;
They clove our barns
They smote the hearth spaces
Of our compounds
They lit previously quenched fuses,
They left dormant mines
At Nsukka, Ulli,
At Asaba, Umuahia, Bonny.

The homesteads abandoned in this century's brush fire witness it:
The myriad eyes of deserted corn cobs in burning barns witness it.

Ask Oba Ovonramwen of Benin
Undone by the curiosity
Of one importunate officer
Who died a blanched monstrosity;
His death burst over the rainforest
In wet wash, devil of leper spores
Whose black pepper of mixed-in shot
Scorched civil out of stranger wars.

Colonists dart back and forth
On termitarium tennis courts.

VIII

The road is demanding, May or September
It asks you to consider your freight,
The principles you must remember,
The sequiturs you must forget.
The palm tree food chain, ivory coast,

Gold coast, embarras de richesses:
All these parallel cosmoses
Can only be borne with a lightened purse.
The future will tell what you've recalled
From what you've wisely set aside.
The Delta downstream will tell what you've recalled
From what you've wisely set aside.

I then, what have I have set aside?
The fall of my friendships
The call of romances
The caul over beginnings
The pall over endings
The small of offences
The drawl of forgiveness
The gall of aryan prejudice
The thrall of Négritude
The stall of juju market
The ball shot from gunboat
The sprawl of mosaic myth
The tall of Iroko-man tales
The shawl of my spread clans
The wall of boarding school bounds
The all of my expanded world
The crawl of new city traffic
The drawl of elderly advice
The drama in stockpiled science...

The drawl from the drool in a mouth full of drug
Is the toothless drawl of words
Which do not also serve as food.
Spit them out.
Must I? Must I spit them out?

Have I let that drawl like ókrò soup
Between the tines,
Over the clammy goddams of my gums?
Or have I swallowed only what what my fists can hold,
Heeding wisdom that it's better to eat by one, right hand?

Left hand, god hand,
Devil hand across Chaos.

So much that's made me who I am
Has found this way's ditch,
More has been scoured by dust devils,
Scratched off as I age and itch
But no more than I my proper self allow;
Enough that I can sense
The creep of tides into deep green,
The grinning mouth, fertile, which inhales/
Exhales grace and mocks all
Desperation after grace.

If you are anchored on solid land, mon semblable,
You can watch my progress.
I drift past. I rush past.
I find stillness. I become very still.

What for this pen in my hand?
It signs the mortgage against my own humanity.
May the crop from these seedling words redeem it.

Such bounty! Oh the delta's hand
Turned purulent by crude demand.

IX

We paint Port Harcourt two faces,
The garden city, the rotting queen—

Pools of rubbish in Rainbow Town;
Her Mami-Wata mangrove daughters
Soak up as much horror as they
Where brown flows maze with green
Where tumble meets tide,
Where silt meets salt,
Where steel meets earth,
Crude pumps meet tumba,
Trumpet meets twin-tone flute.

Even nymphs have limits;
They cry quite out from tribulation,
Clamoring aloud to parent gods.

How fitting that here in Port Harcourt,
Near the river's shunt to infinity,
The cosmos has evolved these questions
Through me, untroubled by humility,
Laozi's decree of chi spells breadth
Of life as my own chí spells soul;
Atma me into brahma flow,
My fractured parts to godhead whole.

Oh this river knows that Gao law
Sparks market riots in Igboland,
That deadly poison in Bamako
Is sweetmeat in the Samarkand.
Ńchéfù Road is no flowered path
To splendent-robed enlightenment;
It holds opposite-wise science,
A school of ruined environment.

This river knows Tombouctou groove
Goes juju mix in Lokoja
That Fulani cattle on the commons

Make for war in Ogoja.
Ñchéfù Road brings you no news
Until you learn to read its swirls
For future blend and batter from
A panoply of local worlds.

X

Only elephant can bloodlessly haul
Hippopotamus from the river
Only the poet can bloodlessly haul
Hippopotamus from the river
The poet befriends elephant
Who makes good on the feat
Even wrestler adept falls weak,
And stung in disgrace and defeat
Calls out for hunter adept.

Legend adept knows to ally
With giants against the wrestler
To speak a sage peace, then lie
A lump in the Niger's sweep,
Unfailing rock, the Niger's poet,
Floating in all the adept's wealth,
Furthermore tripled at this point,
Grace of the wager winnings, holding
Nothing more firmly than the waves
Which rush by, a rock, beholding
The course of all crucial matters
As they rush by, noting the useless
Thrashing limbs of wrestler
As they rush by, tangled in useless
Thrashing limbs of coup plotters
As they rush by, tangled in useless
Thrashing limbs of Mungo Park
Who sought to swallow a river.

He for dey perambulate and for still dey
(Same, same place)
He for dey perambulate and for still dey
(Same, same place)

Ńchéfù Road holds useless
The limbs of those who have come
For high lore and splendent robes;
They shall find themselves overcome
In tides of hippopotamus
And elephant, bundled downstream
With wrestlers and hunters,
With those in the sprawling scheme
Of counter-natural conquest,
Haughty explorers, coup plotters,
Oil men and Hydroengineers
Who shall lie inhumed in these waters.

Let me to strand of the bank
To go nude of shift and resentment
That I lie, a lump in the Niger's sweep—
In hippopotamus contentment.
Unfailing rock, the Niger's poet
To lie, a lump in the Niger's sweep—
While crucial things come rushing by
To lie, a lump in the Niger's sweep—
While useless limbs come thrashing by
Nude of shift and resentment
To lie, a lump in the Niger's sweep—
Hippopotamus contentment.

Cast off your bearings, off your load,
For progress down Ńchéfù Road.

NOTES

I Azikiwe

Page 6: Canal

- Chí—Igbo concept of the self-spirit, similar in idea to the soul.

Page 10: Ọpụ̀tá na Ọ́mụ̀gwọ́

- ọ́mụ̀gwọ́—Igbo: customary four traditional week (16 day) period after a child is born when the father honors the mother with feasts and gifts, and during which the grandmother or in-law visits to take care of the household so the new mother can rest and bond with the baby, also less specifically the traditional six months or so breastfeeding period.
- ọpụ̀tá na ọ́mụ̀gwọ́—Igbo: emerging from ọ́mụ̀gwọ́, the end of the ọ́mụ̀gwọ́ period, which is also the customary naming ceremony for the child.
- Umune, Kálù, Àlà—Igbo gods (Àlà and Umune are goddesses).
- Abagana, Ohafia, Arochukwu—Igbo towns.
- Ụ́mụ̀ ńné—Igbo: literally "mother's people".
- Umon—Narrator's maternal ancestral tongue.
- Ikot Ana—Narrator's maternal home town.
- ọ́párá—Igbo: first born son.
- Ụ́mụ̀nakanù—name of narrator's paternal home town, with the literal Igbo meaning "may the children exceed the parent" ("ụ́mụ̀ na aka únù").
- ọ̀fọ́—Igbo ritual staff of authority, as well as its cosmic source.

Page 14: Colossus

- Chí ya di na m̀bá—(Igbo) his soul, his self-spirit, is at the homestead.

Page 15: Ụ̀mụ̀ Dí Ụ̀zụ́ (Smith's Posterity)

- díké—warrior/scout. dí ụ̀zụ́—blacksmith. dí ákụ́kọ́—storyteller, griot.
- ákụ́lụ́-ákụ́lụ́—Igbo: excess ornamentation.
- díbị̀à—Igbo: general adept of religion, ritual and healing.

Page 19: Electron Microscopy

- Ụ̀mụ̀nakanù—name of narrator's paternal home town, with the literal Igbo meaning "may the children exceed the parent".

Page 23: Why should I Murmur?

- ḿmírí—Igbo: water; body of water.

Page 29: Mysteries of Harvest: Home

- ụ́gụ́—(Igbo) pumpkin vine leaf used in many traditional soups and stews ugu (telfaria occidentalis). often planted alongside yams for Nitrogen fixation.

Page 30: Two Kitchens

- ụ̀tázị̀—Igbo vegetable leaf with bitter flavoring ground and used in soups and for medicine.

II Ojukwu

Page 34: Ǹzọ̀gbú-Ǹzọ̀gbú

- ényí—(Igbo) elephant.
- ényì—(Igbo) friend. Note this is a completely different word from ényí, thanks to Igbo's tonal nature, and one would never be confused with another by an Igbo.
- Ényíḿbà Ényí/Ǹzọ̀gbú—Igbo war chant meaning, approximately "Elephant, the masses, march on and trample the enemy".
- nwókè—(Igbo) man.

- nwányǐ—(Igbo) woman.
- jí—(Igbo) yam (proper Dioscorea yam, not sweet potato).
- kwanu—(Igbo) intensifying or as in this case interrogatory particle, a bit like denn in german.
- òbí—(Igbo) central space of a household compound. Also used metonymically to connote brave, virile youth. In the northern Onitsha dialect a name for a ruler.
- Omo-Shasha, Oluwa, North Cross River, Kamuku or Yankari— forest or game reserves in Nigeria, mostly with elephant sanctuaries.
- Tùfiákwà! Ọwú árụ́rụ́ àlà—(Igbo) expression of violent disgust with the abomination of what's happened.

Page 42: Mysteries of Harvest II

- Ahiajioku—Igbo goddess who personifies yam cultivation— true Discorea yams, not sweet potatoes—the bedrock of Igbo culture.
- úgú—(Igbo) pumpkin vine leaf used in many traditional soups and stews ugu (telfaria occidentalis). often planted alongside yams for Nitrogen fixation.
- Ijaw, Arochukwu, Abiriba, Ohafia—Southern Nigerian peoples and towns which became involved with the trans-Atlantic slave trade.
- Àlà—The great Igbo mother goddess who personifies the earth. Shares elements with Gaia and Demeter.

III Okigbo

Page 57: Éké

- n'úzò—(Igbo) over the roads.
- éké—(Igbo) python (Python regius), a very sacred animal.
- òbí—(Igbo) domicile, household compound.
- Chúkwú—(Igbo) supreme deity.
- ńzú—(Igbo) chalk.

- Nwa Ímò m̀mírí, nwa Dím Ònyékà íyí—Narrator's relationship to ancestral rivers.
- Ụ̀bụ̀bọ̀-m̀múọ́—(Igbo) vengeance from the spirit world.

Page 65: Le Freak Musique Afrique

- èkpè, nri—(Igbo) Left, right.
- ọ̀jà—(Igbo) traditional hollow-reed flute.
- ùdù—(Igbo) drum with a resonant "talking effect".
- úgú—(Igbo) pumpkin vine leaf (telfaria occidentalis) used in many traditional soups and stews.
- díbịà—(Igbo) general adept of religion, ritual and healing.

Page 68: Two-Voiced Flute

- Ímò m̀mírí—Great river of the author's home state; m̀mírí is Igbo for water.
- Biafara—early name of the SE Nigeria and W Cameroon region.

Page 72: Fortune of Chí

- Chí—Igbo concept of the self-spirit, similar in idea to the soul.

Page 73: Road to Onitsha, 1989

- Onitsha (Onishe)—City on the banks of the river Niger in southeast Nigeria, gateway to the west of the country and commercial center of the Igbo people.
- ị màgo—Igbo, colloquial, approximately: "you know, now".
- Agbero—Nigerian pidgin slang (from Yoruba) for an "area boy," a young man who takes on odd jobs around marketplaces or other public areas, including touting for transport passengers, and reputedly including criminal activity.

Page 79: Rainbow City Presage of Storm

- ìchékú, iroko, údárà—Trees commonly found in Igbo land. Ìchékú is a variety of tamarind (Dialium Guineense or tamarindus indica). Ụ́dárà (Chrysophylum africanum) is known for its tart-sweet, moist, fleshy fruit.

Page 82: Igbo Directions in Amsterdam

- Kèdú ka í mèrè?—Igbo: how are you doing?
- Ọ̀ dị̀ ḿmá!—Igbo: it is well.
- Anioma—Territory just west of the Niger from Igboland, whose people are either Igbo or closely related.
- Á nàm a chọ́ọ́—Igbo: I'm looking for.
- Ọ̀ nwèrè ónyé na e nyèlúm áká ébáà-hu—Igbo: Someone there is to do me a favor.
- Bíkò, i nwéére íhé díkà map?—Please, do you have any sort of map?
- Onishe—Northwestern Igbo goddess and personification of the River Niger, source of the city name Onitsha.
- jí—(Igbo) yam (proper Dioscorea yam, not sweet potato).

Page 85: Prayer Before Writing

- chí na álúsí—Igbo—my personal spirit, plus all other great spirits.
- ébí ógwù: Igbo—porcupine (Hystrix cristata).

IV Ńchéfù Road

Page 87: Ńchéfù Road

- ǹchéfù—Igbo: forgetting, amnesia.
- shīfu—Chinese master.
- Ímò and Íyí—Important Igboland rivers, with íyí a generic term for a body of water.
- Ékpè and Ágbàrà—Cardinal spirits of Igbo land, particularly south, near Arochukwu, and north, near Nsukka.
- Pángŭ—Chinese god and goddess of creation, embodiment of the cosmos emerged from chaos, embodiment of yin and yang.
- ókrò—Vegetable seed pod indigenous to Igbo land (Hibiscus esculenta), called okra in English.
- tumba—Large Yoruba native drum, popular in many Black cultures.
- Oyono—Traditional Efik name for the Cross River.

ACKNOWLEDGMENTS

I thank Mel Pryor for selecting this manuscript for the Christopher Smart Prize. I thank Todd Swift, Amira Ghanim, and the other editors and staff at The Black Spring Press Group for their time, efforts and care in giving this book a home.

I thank the Boulder County Arts Alliance of Colorado for its support in bringing this book to fruition, through the BCAA Endowment Fellowship.

Poems included in this volume first appeared in the following journals.

- "Fortune of Chi," *Soundzine*, June 2011.
- "Mango Flesh," *Scree Magazine*, February 2012.
- "Two Kitchens", *Gris Gris*, May 2013.
- "Ala Entertains," *Eternal Haunted Summer*, December 2012.
- "Dear Bonny, Dear Biafara," *Don't Just Sit There* (published as "Dear Biafra"), July 2013.
- "Okobi and the Crying...," *Looseleaf Tea*, October 2013.
- "Igbo Directions in Amsterdam," *Literary Bohemian*, November 2014.
- "Rheotype," *Best New African Poets*, December 2015.
- "Road from Calabar to Abuja," *Expound*, September 2015.
- "Two-Voiced Flute," *Opossum*, May 2016.
- "Mysteries of Harvest II," *Whirlwind Magazine*, June 2016.
- "Mysteries of Harvest: Home," *Sirsee*, June 2017.
- "Le Freak Musique Afrique," *Okey Panky*, August 2017.
- "Ogbúnàbàlì and Hypnos, 1949," *Journal of the American Society of Anesthesiologists*, July 2018.